The Chameleon in the Closet

❧

A Conservative Jewish Mother
Reaches Out to Her Orthodox Sons

D1430138

BJ Rosenfeld

While the incidents in this book did happen,
some of the names and places have been changed.

Acknowledgment

I am grateful to Marion Roach Smith, Marita Golden, Juliette Guttman, Honor Moore, Sarah Shapiro, Sandi Gelles-Cole, James Miller, Barry Trachtenberg, Rabbi Yosef Wikler, Tom Jenks, Rob Brill, Miriam Rosenfeld, Margery Diamond Zucker, Doris Calderon, Phyllis Morrison, Deborah Goldstein, and Phillip Lopate, in addition to my family, friends, and everyone else who inspired, encouraged, and helped me along the way.

For Yehuda, Chaim,
Penina, Shulamit
and Peter

A Chameleon's Cluttered Closet

Our older son did not want me to write this book. The story is his, he insisted. But the life-changing decision he made at college continues to impact the way the rest of us live our lives. After turning away from his Jewishness, he met a charismatic Orthodox rabbi and became hooked on traditional Judaism. Yehuda now lives in Jerusalem, wears a black hat, and prays three times a day. His wife dresses modestly and wears a *sheitel*, a wig. Our younger son Chaim found his own brand of traditional Judaism on a tour of Israel while in high school. Would he have become Orthodox if Yehuda hadn't paved the way? No way to tell. Chaim and his family live in metropolitan New York.

While our sons were growing up, I wondered if they would ever stop fighting, what colleges they would get into, and whom they would marry. But I never expected either of them to tell me that my kitchen was not kosher enough. Though the accommodations needed to make them both—but especially Yehuda—feel comfortable in our home have not been easy, I am proud of their dedication to the Judaism of our ancestors. Thanks to them I have had an entrée into the world of *shadchens*, *sheitels*, *vorts*, and *cholent*.

Somewhere along the way I have become a chameleon. I change my clothing and demeanor, not at whim, but to suit the situation and the circumstances. My closet contains two distinct wardrobes: shorts, slacks, and sleeveless tops for the world I live in; long skirts and long-sleeved blouses for the world in which our sons exist.

I love my jeans. The designer ones with flared legs and floral embroidery look great, especially when I top them with the hot pink shell that brightens my complexion. The straight-legged ones give me a sexy silhouette, and the baggy ones with the deep pockets are perfect for hiking. My sons' belief that women must not wear men's clothing and vice versa doesn't stop me from wearing jeans. Just not in their company. I did not always give in so easily. In the early years of Yehuda's religious transformation, he and I would butt heads every so often. I can't remember what the issues were, but they were very important at the time. Now when others ask why I'm so accommodating, my answer is "Why not?" when there are other issues—not watching television, using the phone, or driving the car on *Shabbos*, the Sabbath; not going out to eat because there are no kosher restaurants in our area; and trying to maintain the highest level of kosher standards in my kitchen—that are far more troublesome than putting on a skirt.

Speaking of skirts, I have twenty-five: denim, woolen, linen, cotton-knit, and acrylic; solid colored and floral; pleated, straight and flared; skorts (skirt and shorts combos), minis, midis; ankle-length and floor-length ones that don't come out of my closet unless my sons are around. My favorite is grey polyester with a kick pleat in the front that brushes the front of my ankles and lets me feel feminine, even a little sexy, but still covers me up. It comes along on every trip to Israel—we travel there every few months to visit with Yehuda, his wife Penina, and our seven grandchildren all under the age of eight.

The twelve-hour trip to Israel is tiresome. Being confined in a skirt for that long is unbearable. So I board the plane in a sweat suit, sneakers and socks, and change in the restroom after we land, a feat that sounds simple in principle but even after numerous tries—fourteen at last count—is far from easy to carry out. After staking out the roomiest stall and positioning my carry-on bag flat on the floor with the zipper facing upward, there's barely enough room to stand. No matter, I riffle through a collection of books, makeup, earplugs, eyeshades, left-over snacks, and last-minute gifts for the grandkids, and retrieve my clothes—a freshly ironed rose-colored blouse wrapped in plastic to keep out wrinkles; a black cotton skirt with an elastic waist stretchy enough to be comfortable because I'm always bloated from the flight; a new pack of pantyhose; and a pair of black leather pumps—taking care that nothing drops into the toilet. Removing the sweat suit is done standing, as is putting on both the blouse and skirt. But the pantyhose is more involved. Perching on top of the toilet or straddling my carry-on, I hold myself up with one hand on the wall and try to put on the stockings with the other, a tricky maneuver that involves at least ten minutes of sweat. Finally stuffing my feet into the dress shoes, stowing my sweat suit and sneakers in my bag, and looking around to make sure nothing is left behind, I button the top button of my blouse and say good-bye to my everyday life.

On the way home I do the same thing in reverse. The size of the stall in the ladies room is no longer important because I don't care about wrinkling my clothes. They'll go into the washer at home. As soon as I feel the soft lining of my sweat suit, I start to relax.

I don't know why, but this switch in character often brings to mind the navy blue dress I wore with a strand of pearls the first time my husband Peter and I met our future daughter-in-law. That was over nine years ago, the same day as my father-in-law's eightieth birthday party. My mother told me I looked out of place at the party in a dress. She and the other women were in pants. My mother did not know about my machinations early that morning in front of the mirror, shifting my weight, then sitting down and crossing my legs in an effort to ensure that the hem of my solid-colored dress covered my knees, all in the hope of not embarrassing myself later that day when Peter and I met Penina and her parents.

Penina was twenty-six; Yehuda, twenty-five. She grew up religious; he did not. He had assured her that we were okay with his religiosity, but she would not agree to marry him until she heard the news directly from us.

Their engagement party took place two weeks later. Under normal circumstances, I would have worn red, my favorite color. But Penina and her mother were dressed in navy and charcoal the day we met them. So I riffle. A phone call provided the answer. "Try to cover your elbows, ankles, and collarbone with a neutral color, if you can," was Penina's sug-

2

Beer Did Not Do It

Who would have thought that Yehuda's transformation towards Orthodox Judaism would start out during his freshman year at Princeton University—once known as a hotbed of anti-Semitism? But that's the way it happened. According to posters dotting the campus, the highlight of our first Parents Weekend at Princeton was the Saturday afternoon football game. Indeed, the idea of attending an Ivy League football game—the stadium stuffed with spectators, the rivalry between the two sides, the cheerleaders putting on a show—was definitely an event. But the highlight of my weekend was spending time with Yehuda. Was it only a month ago that Peter and I dropped him off for the start of his freshman year? I missed him so much. The empty feeling lingered every time I walked past his bedroom.

He had spent summers at camp so this was not the first time he lived away from home. I wanted him to have his own life, to be independent. Going away to college was the start. Then again, that meant being on his own with no one looking out for him except the academic advisor he was supposed to check in with once a year. I hoped we had prepared him well enough to face the temptations college had to offer.

Yehuda led us to the stadium with Chaim at his side. Despite the three-year difference in their ages, they were almost the same height. For once they seemed to be getting along until Chaim jabbed Yehuda in the ribs one too many times. Luckily, we were able to separate them before Yehuda, who earned a black belt in karate, was able to do any harm.

On the way up the steep stadium steps, I asked Yehuda if he would join Hillel, a Jewish campus organization.

"After all the youth group meetings you made me go to in high school, I've had enough of all that," he said, his dark brown eyes glaring into mine.

I suddenly felt guilty. Had I done too much or not enough?

Once we reached our seats, Yehuda told us he was rushing a fraternity.

"They're really great guys," he said smiling so broadly that his double dimples were clearly visible. "They've got a keg around here somewhere. I don't want to disappoint them."

He left his seat four times, returning ten minutes later. The stale smell of beer on his breath reminded me of when he was fifteen. Peter and I came home early one evening only to be greeted by empty beer bottles on the kitchen counter and the sound of riotous laughter from the family room. Yehuda insisted the beer had not been his idea. "It happened somehow" was his explanation, but he would not say whose idea it was. I was furious but knew better than to embarrass him in front of his friends. Instead, Peter and I went upstairs and called the other parents.

Waiting for the parents to pick up their kids, Peter told me, "I wondered when something like this would happen."

I was incredulous.

"You sound as if you wanted it to happen," I said.

"It's what teenage boys do," he said, nodding. "You have to expect them to try to push the limits sometime."

I thought of the boys in the ninth grade Spanish class I taught at the high school, who were always trying to see what they could get away with. Yehuda had never been like that. His teachers had only good things to say about him, such as how deeply he thought things out before he spoke and what a wonderful student he was. Of course he and I had our conflicts. His room was a mess. He played his stereo too loud. It was hard to wake him up in the morning. But this was the first time he really disappointed me.

"Underage drinking may be normal, but that doesn't make it a good idea," I told Peter.

"Doesn't stop it from being a rite of passage," Peter said.

And then there were the beer parties Yehuda and his buddies often held in the field within walking distance of our house. I once tried to talk him out of going—not only on account of the underage drinking but because I was afraid a car might run him down. It should not have surprised me when he said I could not stop him. He was probably correct about me trying to baby him. But he was still my child, and it was hard to let him do things I considered dangerous. I never fell asleep on those Saturday nights until after I heard him come home.

I had no doubt that Yehuda would get into the fraternity at Princeton, but the anguish in his voice was unmistakable when he told us they turned him down. I felt helpless, wishing there was something I could do to make him feel better but he was despondent. Telling him he should have had a second-choice fraternity would not have helped. Princeton had been his first and only choice. And he had been accepted early.

It took Yehuda a long time to recover from his first major rejection.

Now and then I wonder what my life would be like today if he had joined that fraternity.

Yehuda's major was computer science. I never expected him to take a Judaic studies elective, but he did just that during his second semester. He told us it was a prerequisite for a summer job at Camp Ramah, a Jewish overnight camp in the Berkshires, but I hoped it would pique his interest in learning more about our religion.

I have to be careful what I wish for.

A few weeks into his second semester, Yehuda started eating his meals at the Center for Jewish Life on campus.

"How's the food?" I asked him, trying not to sound too excited.

"Not half bad," he said, "Even if it is kosher."

I did not bother reminding him that our house was kosher.

"Must be a great place to meet Jewish girls," Peter told him.

"I eat there because it's convenient. Same building as Judaic studies."

"How's that going?" I asked, hopefully.

"I hated Hebrew as a kid, but this is different. We use it to analyze a portion of the *Torah*. I never knew there was so much I did not know about my own religion."

Even as I hoped that Yehuda's fascination with Judaism would continue, I never expected him to participate in Friday night and Saturday morning religious services. But he did. It was tempting to call the Judaic studies professor to thank him. After discussing this with Peter, I decided to wait and see how long our son's newly found religious commitment might last.

As time went on, Yehuda started to change. He used to have a wonderful sense of humor, never at a loss for words. There was so much he used to share with us: the parties, the rock concerts. It was hard to tell if he was just growing up or if it was something else. Whatever it was, I did not like it.

A typical conversation was as follows:

"How's it going?" I asked Yehuda.

"Okay," he replied.

"Got a lot of papers to write this week?"

"Not really."

"Need any money?" asked Peter.

"No thanks."

Peter tried one of his corny jokes. "Did I tell you the one about the two men who went to the deli?"

"No thanks."

Yehuda had not been home for two months.

"Any plans this weekend?" I asked. "Mind if we come for a visit?"

"I'll be at Rabbi Katz's."

"The guy who teaches Judaic studies?"

"He's not just a guy," Yehuda said, emphatically. "Rabbi Katz is an Orthodox rabbi."

"You there last weekend?" Peter said.

"What if I was?"

"He'll forgive you for spending time with your family," I said, hoping to sound more confident than I felt.

Silence.

"Dad and I love you very much."

"Talk to you next week."

Yehuda hung up.

I sat staring at the phone. I used to be able to anticipate the changes our sons would undergo. Why was Yehuda spending so much time with that Orthodox rabbi? Why did it seem that the more he learned about his Jewish heritage, the less he shared with us? What exactly was he learning in that class?

If I phoned that rabbi, would I learn more about my son?

At the end of an hour, during which I cried, wrote, crossed out, rewrote, and rehearsed a list of questions I hoped to ask Yehuda's rabbi, I went downstairs and found Peter reading the newspaper.

"How can you be so relaxed?" I asked.

"It's Sunday," Peter said. "Why not?"

"Yehuda's acting so strange. How do we know he hasn't been brainwashed?"

"Just going through a stage."

"I can't help thinking about the Moonies ... Jim Jones ... and what happened in Waco, Texas. How do we know that Orthodox rabbi doesn't head up his own religious cult?"

"He'll snap out of it by the end of the semester."

"Then it may be too late," I said, handing him the pad on which I'd written the questions. "Look this over and tell me if I've left anything out."

He glanced at the list. "Looks good to me."

"How come I'm the only one who's worried about the change in Yehuda?"

"Because I don't let myself get worked up about things I can't control."

It was so hard to let go. Sitting on the edge of my desk chair, I tried to compose myself. What if the rabbi refused to talk to me? I had to take a chance. After dialing the rabbi's number that was listed in the university directory, I braced myself for whatever came next.

"Hello," said a pleasant-sounding male voice. "This is Rabbi Katz."

Clearing my throat several times, I then introduced myself.

"I'm pleased you called," the rabbi said. "Yehuda's one of my best students."

The rabbi sounded nicer than I expected. He even seemed happy to hear from me.

Having been raised to treat all rabbis with respect, I resisted the impulse to ask the first question on my list: What did you do to my son? Instead, I asked about the Judaic studies course.

"It's really an outreach program," the rabbi said, sounding matter-of-fact.

"What's that?"

"I don't have to tell you that college is a time for exploration and experimentation for our young people." I nodded silently. "For some, it's a candy store with too many choices." That reminded me of a roommate who flunked out after spending time partying instead of studying. The rabbi went on. "I'm trying to keep as many as possible of our Jewish students from being tempted by other religions."

I pictured my cousin who was fluent in Hebrew, but turned to Buddhism at college and then distanced himself from the rest of the family. I did not want that to happen to Yehuda.

I started to pace.

"Yehuda's not thinking of becoming a Buddhist, is he?"

"You have nothing to worry about. He's too busy discovering the beauty of his own heritage."

I stopped pacing.

"How come he's so remote?"

"He's still finding his way, processing what he's learned so far."

That made sense.

"Why is it the more he learns, the less he's willing to share with us?"

"He's probably unsure how you'll react to his becoming more religious than the way he grew up. He's thinking of becoming a *ba'al teshuvah*." I did not like the way that sounded. "A *ba'al teshuvah* is a non-observant Jew who turns to traditional observant Judaism."

"So Yehuda wants to become . . . Orthodox?"

"That's the idea."

I considered myself a good Conservative Jew, but I had never met anyone who was Orthodox.

"Why ... why would he think we'd be upset if he became ... Orthodox?"

"You do sound a bit stressed."

"It's just that—."

"Don't let yourself get worked up. He's got a good head on his shoulders. He'll open up once he realizes you still love and accept him."

When Yehuda and Chaim were little, they were usually the last ones picked for sports. Other kids gave them a hard time for getting good grades. At times like that I used to tell them, "I love you just the way you are." That seemed to help. Maybe Yehuda needed to hear those words again.

I tried to find a tactful way to ask my next question but blurted out, "How come Yehuda spends so much time at your house?"

"He's learning first-hand how our Orthodox family puts religious observance into practice. By the way, my wife and I would be more than happy to have your family spend a *Shabbos* with us."

I was not sure we would ever take him up on his offer but thanked him and added, "But it won't be for a while. Yehuda hasn't been home for ages."

It's hard to believe I was so naïve in accepting the rabbi's assurances with no concept of the struggles that might lie ahead.

When I told Peter about my conversation with Rabbi Katz, he said, "I told you Yehuda would never join a cult. But you didn't believe me."

"Kids change," I said. "Look how naïve I was before I met you."

"Aren't you glad I expanded your horizons?"

The next day it was a pleasure to hear a message from Yehuda on our answering machine saying that he planned to come home the following weekend. Maybe my conversation with Rabbi Katz was all it took. I could not wait to call Peter with the good news.

"He's really coming home?" Peter asked.

"I can't wait!" I practically shouted into the phone.

"Me neither."

Many secular Jews are offended by what they consider to be the narrowness and fundamentalism of the Orthodox Jews. These secular Jews consider themselves enlightened; they consider the Orthodox, with their many traditions and commandments, old-fashioned and narrow-minded. One might ask how it's possible that a group of people that faced prejudice for thousands of years and suffered through the Holocaust during the past century can harbor feelings of resentment toward their fellow Jews. Not only is this possible, it's constantly there beneath the surface of Semitic relations. The real question for secular Jews should be, if it's okay to live next door to Christians, why can't you live peacefully next door to a neighbor who observes *Shabbos*?

It's no secret that every Jew believes that his or her brand of Judaism—Orthodox, Conservative, Reform, Reconstructionist, or un-affiliated—is superior to all the rest. Although many non-observant Jews like nothing better than "a good kosher-style corned beef on rye," they would never consider entering a kosher restaurant for fear that some of the "Old World traditions" might rub off.

Kosher food is not blessed by a rabbi. To be considered kosher, food has to conform to a set of dietary laws that date back to biblical times and specify which foods are permitted to be eaten and which are not. Fruits and vegetables are kosher. Fish that have fins and scales are kosher, but shellfish is not. Cows are kosher; pigs are not.

Jews often have a complicated relationship with keeping kosher. Many of my friends grew up in kosher homes, just as I did, but few keep kosher today. Some kept up the tradition for a while after they were married, others abandoned it as soon as they moved away from home. Even those of us who still keep kosher do so in our own fashion.

I never thought my sons would tell me my kitchen was not kosher enough. But they insinuated as much, asking me to let them strip my cupboards of anything that ever came in touch with food—including pots, pans, dishes, glassware, and cutlery—and bring it all to the *mikvah*.

From *The Ritual Bath*, a mystery by Faye Kellerman about a murder that took place in a *mikvah*, I knew that a *mikvah* was a specially constructed ritual pool for women.

What did that have to do with my dishes?

"Where are you going again? " I asked my sons.

"The *mikvah*," they said, as if they were doing me a favor.

"Why?"

"To *toivel* everything."

"Why?'

"So it's kosher."

"The only food I cook is kosher."

My tone of voice must have gotten to them because they stopped to explain that before something can be used with food, it first has to be immersed in a *mikvah*.

"The same one women use?"

"Of course not! There's a separate one for utensils."

"How was I supposed to know if you did not tell me?"

"Sorry, Mom," they said, surrounding me with a hug.

When shopping for groceries, I started carrying an index card that showed the *hechshers*, kosher symbols, I'm supposed to check. Needless to say this limits my food-buying options. When in doubt, I called the Kosher Hot Line. I've called so often that they jokingly offered me a "frequent caller card." It was easy to find most of the ingredients I needed at a local grocery, but the rest had to be purchased at a supermarket about a half-hour from our home. So I learned to stock up. Buying a product I used to enjoy that did not carry the correct kosher marking was clearly a temptation, but I would not do that. Yehuda was not going to go over everything in our pantry. It was a matter of trust. I wanted him to feel comfortable in our home, even if I thought he was going a bit overboard.

Initially, the preparation of holiday meals—which I loved—lost some of its charm and was replaced by self-induced stress. The kitchen was no longer my domain. It seemed as if my every move was being watched. Before starting a recipe I had prepared with ease in the past,

I felt the need to consult with my sons, who appreciated my efforts, patiently answered all my questions, and reminded me that learning was an on-going process. It was okay to make a mistake.

For the first five years of their marriage, one of my friends had a steady date with her husband every Thursday night. They met after work at their favorite kosher butcher shop—at that time there were four to choose from in downtown Albany—and stocked up for the following week. This ritual continued even after they bought a home in the suburbs thirty miles away. But by the time their first child was born, my friend's husband was too busy at work to spend time at the butcher, and the harsh winter weather, in addition to the forty-five minute drive with the new baby, the icy Albany streets, and the impossible parking situation, proved to be too much for my friend to go by herself.

Although she stopped buying kosher meat, she could not bring herself to disregard the dietary restrictions of not mixing meat and milk. Cheeseburgers were out of the question. She gave her kids soda whenever they had meat. Not until the pediatrician insisted that they needed more calcium did my friend start giving her kids milk along with their meatballs. Even then she found the idea so revolting that, as soon as the milk was poured, she dashed out of the kitchen, often leaving the three of them to take care of themselves.

Another friend, who does not keep kosher, told me how hard it was to keep everything straight when she and her husband spent a month living in someone else's kosher home while that family was out of town. Though the owners had labeled the meat and dairy cabinets and had written out detailed instructions on keeping kosher, confusion set in when it was time to empty the dishwasher. One night, my friend stopped herself just as she was about to pour Parmesan dressing on her salad which was in a meat dish. What to do, she wondered. Her solution was ingenious, if not exactly kosher. Instead of giving up her favorite salad dressing, she put the salad in a dairy bowl on a dairy placemat along with a dairy fork, and placed her steak on a meat plate along with a meat fork. Then the meal proceeded without a hitch.

Still another friend told me that her parents used to have three sets of dishes: one for meat, one for dairy, and a glass set for Chinese food. Although the parents gave up on kosher after moving to Florida, my friend considers them hypocrites for having brought nonkosher food into their home. That is why she decided not to have a kosher home of her own.

As Rabbi Jack Moline said in *Growing Up Jewish*, "Everyone who keeps kosher will tell you that his version is the only correct version. Everyone else is either a fanatic or a heretic." I guess it depends on whom you ask.

I could never see myself not keeping a kosher home. Yet I am far from kosher when it comes to eating out. There are no kosher restaurants where we live. When left with a choice of making allowances or never eating out, I pick the first option. My parents took me to nonkosher restaurants when I was growing up, but I never ate lobster until Peter insisted I try it. Even then, I refused to touch the shell, so after spearing the meat Peter handed over my fork.

Does keeping kosher at home and eating non-kosher out make me conflicted? Do I feel like a hypocrite? No. I am doing what works for me.

The other day, a friend complained that her Orthodox cousins have no problem sleeping in her beds and eating kosher take-out on paper plates in her dining room, but boycotted her daughter's wedding to a non-Jewish man.

"They talked about wonderful weddings on their side of the family but refused to come to my daughter's," my friend lamented. "Never met anyone so narrow-minded! Why couldn't they just be happy for me that my daughter was marrying a wonderful man? What about love? Do they believe in that? We make allowances for them. Why can't they do the same thing for us?"

What could I do but listen? There was no way she would see it from her cousins' perspective. Trying to get her to understand that intermarriage is forbidden in the Orthodox world would have been wasting my breath. On second thought, it would have fired her up even more.

Another friend said her mother lives in Brooklyn in an apartment building where most of the tenants are Orthodox. The other day, a three-year-old yelled at my friend's mother for carrying a handbag on *Shabbos*. Situations like that helped convince my friend that the Orthodox are biased against those who are not.

"As if we're not as good as they are because we bend the rules," she said.

Once I would have said that three-year-old was out of line. Now that I have Orthodox grandchildren, I just listened to my friend. My three-year-old granddaughter might be tempted to yell at someone carrying a handbag on *Shabbos*, but I'm pretty sure she wouldn't do it. My son and daughter-in law teach their children that "different people do different things" and that they should be patient with people who don't know the rules.

According to the Orthodox tradition of dressing modestly, Penina wears tights or opaque knee-highs even in the hot weather. I often go barelegged.

A few years ago, I was sitting on the floor doing a puzzle with one of my granddaughters—who happened to be five at the time—when she gently rubbed my bare leg and asked, "Bubbe, why don't you wear tights like Mommy?"

If I told her the truth, would that be enough? I wondered.

"Because I don't want to," I said, smiling.

"Oh," she said and went back to the puzzle.

In an ideal world, all Jews would get along. But that's not the way it is. The "black hat fanatics"—as the Orthodox are known to some in the world of secular Judaism—and the "ignorant bigots"—the label many Orthodox use to describe the secular Jews—are equally guilty of antagonism toward each other. Many non-observant Jews don't understand why every Jew would not want to be just like them. Many pious Jews feel the same way

Friday was only four days away. There was so much I wanted to do to make Yehuda's homecoming absolutely perfect. I made a list: straighten his room—not that he would notice, but it mattered to me;

plan the meals; buy the groceries; do the cooking. I decided to prepare his favorites: vegetable soup, brisket, oven-roasted potatoes, tossed salad, and apple crisp.

Mulling over the recipes, I found myself wondering whether Yehuda's newfound religious fervor had an impact on his clothing. The last time he was home, he wore nothing but his favorite pair of frayed jeans along with T-shirts imprinted with beer logos. I hoped he would continue bringing home his dirty laundry. Though it was hard to find time to wash it, the smell of his sweat-soaked socks made me feel closer to him.

After we heard the garage door moan, Peter and I watched our sons give each other a bear hug, their usual greeting. Yehuda's wavy dark brown hair was cut short, and parted to the side, in contrast with Chaim's disheveled, brown curls that reached to his shoulders. Yehuda was still lanky; his younger brother had increased in bulk. We separated them as soon as the bear hug started turning into a wrestling hold.

Patting an overstuffed duffle bag obviously filled with dirty laundry, Yehuda smiled saying, "Mom, I brought you a present."

"I'll do it after dinner," I smiled back.

"Would you mind waiting till tomorrow night?" he asked. "It's better not to use the washer or dryer until after *Shabbos*."

I was about to ask him for an explanation but the oven timer went off. So I went to check on dinner.

From the kitchen, I heard Yehuda and Chaim dragging a suitcase upstairs. Within seconds, rock music blasted my eardrums. I guessed things hadn't changed that much,

Before we sat down to eat, I lit the *Shabbos* candles and Peter said the blessings over the wine and the *challah*—rituals that felt like old friends.

When Yehuda was still living at home we had a festive *Shabbos* meal every Friday night. Now I was out of practice because after Yehuda started college, Chaim, a high school sophomore, convinced me that going out to our local pizza parlor was a cool thing to do on Friday nights.

Chaim still had on the ketchup-stained tee shirt and jeans he wore to school. Yehuda was wearing a long-sleeved white shirt and black dress pants.

"How come you're all dressed up?" I asked Yehuda.

"It's important to look nice for *Shabbos*," he said.

I glanced at Peter who was wearing jeans and a blue plaid shirt. Thank goodness I still had on the dress I had worn to work. Why did I feel that way? I now ask myself. Yehuda was dressed up, but in no way did that mean the rest of us had to follow suit.

Compared to when we spoke on the phone, Yehuda seemed more relaxed. He even listened attentively to Chaim's complaints about the long research papers he had to do.

"I thought that stuff was a stupid waste of time," Yehuda told his brother. "But some friends said it would get me ready for college."

"Okay," Chaim grumbled. "I'll do them."

It was good to feel like a family of four again.

"Is *Shabbos* like this at the Katz's?" I asked.

Shaking his head, Yehuda said, "With six kids, their house is much noisier."

"What I meant was, what kind of food do they have?"

"Mrs. Katz makes lots of stuff: *kugels*, vegetables, brisket, chicken, potatoes, rice, and a few desserts." I started to wonder if I should have prepared more food until Yehuda added, as he helped himself to an-other serving of apple crisp, "Mom, I sure missed your cooking."

When everyone was finished eating, I started clearing the table. But Yehuda gestured for me to sit back down.

"Sorry," he said, "I need some time to *bensch*."

"What?" Chaim asked.

"To recite the blessing after meals we learned in Sunday school," Yehuda explained. "That's *bensching*."

Shrugging his shoulders, Chaim said, "Don't take too long. There's a new TV show."

"No TV for me until after *Shabbos*."

"Why not?"

"*Shabbos* is supposed to be a day of rest," Yehuda said. I could tell he was trying hard not to sound condescending.

"Watching TV's not what I'd call work," said Chaim, checking his watch. "Speed it up. The show's on in twenty minutes."

Yehuda took a small prayer book out of his pocket, searched for the right page, and started chanting in Hebrew, emphasizing each word as if every syllable were precious:

"*Baw-rooch ah-taw A-do-noi, Ello-hay-noo me-lech haw-o-lawm, ha-zan es ha'ol-um ku-lo bi-tu-vo bi-chain, bi-che-sed, ov-ra-cha-mim. . .*"

(Blessed are You, O Lord our God, King of all the world, Who feeds the whole world with goodness, with grace, with loving kindness, and with mercy. . .)

I closed my eyes, picturing myself at the age of five sitting at my grandparents' table, listening intently while Pop *bensched*. I did not understand any of the words, but Nana made me sit still until he was done. Back then, I assumed it was just something my grandfather did. Now my older son was doing the same thing.

3

The Strudel Connection

I was three years old when my mother went to work and left me in the loving care of my grandparents, Nana and Pop. Their one-bedroom apartment—upstairs from the sporting goods store they owned in my hometown of Glen Cove, New York—became my second home.

Nana never yelled at me, never made me feel I was not good enough. She had dark brown eyes and shiny grey hair streaked with silver that she rolled up in a bun. I felt closer to her than anyone else. She used to tell me stories about growing up in Russia, and about the pogroms that forced her family to emigrate from Russia. She was always telling me that her happiest times were spent with me.

One of my fondest memories was "helping" Nana make strudel. We sifted flour into a bowl, cracked some eggs into a glass to check for blood spots—which would have made them unkosher, therefore unusable—and then used a wooden spoon to mix the dough. I loved feeling Nana's fingers on mine as we guided the rolling pin over the dough. For the filling, we mixed cinnamon, sugar, lemon juice, walnuts, dried fruit, and plenty of wheat germ. Proper nutrition was important to Nana, so she added wheat germ to everything. Once the dough was covered with a layer of filling, we carefully rolled it into a log, placed it on a cookie sheet, and then into the oven.

Long before the pastry turned crisp and golden brown, the familiar fragrance filled the air. The hardest part was the long wait for the strudel to cool. Nana would not let me have any until we sliced it, placed some on a serving plate covered with waxed paper, and stored the rest in a cream-colored ceramic canister that had a picture of an apple and the word "COOKIES" painted on the front. The scent of cinnamon still lingers in that canister, the largest of a set of five that I now proudly display on my own kitchen counter.

Looking up at my grandmother, who was wiping off her hands on her homemade blue and red plaid apron, I asked, "Please may I have some, now?"

Nana smiled and gestured toward the kitchen table covered with a plastic floral tablecloth. "Of course, darling," she always said. I can still see the dimples in her cheeks. "As soon as you sit down. Eating while you're standing up is bad for your digestion."

The brown vinyl seat of the metal kitchen chair squished under me. We had a routine. Nana poured a glass of milk, placed the platter of strudel in front of me, filled the kettle with water, and set it to boil on the stove. By the time her tea was finished steeping in a water glass, I was already savoring my second slice of strudel. Finally, Nana perched on the edge of a chair—in case Pop needed her to rush down the fire escape in the back of the building to help him in the store—and started sipping her tea through the cube of sugar placed between her teeth.

"Aren't you going to have any?" I asked.

Nana inspected the platter and picked up one slice. "Well, maybe just one," she would say and take a bite. "If I'm not careful, I'm going to have to go on a reducing diet." I did not know why she said this so often. I always thought she looked just right.

Nana followed the kosher dietary laws, especially the one that forbids mixing meat and dairy. She had two refrigerators, one on either side of the kitchen door: the larger one, *milchig* (dairy); the older, smaller one, *fleishig* (meat). Any leftovers from a meat meal, including cooked vegetables, went into the fleishig ice box. Food that was *pareve* (neither meat nor dairy), like eggs, fresh fruits or vegetables, and a large plastic container of assorted vitamins, was stored in the *milchig* one. Two white porcelain sinks in the kitchen—each rimmed in speckled red Formica that matched the countertops—took up almost an entire wall. Each one had its own cover so that the entire area could be used for either meat or dairy. Nana kept her two sets of cutlery, dishes, and pots in the white wooden cupboards on opposite sides of the room.

On Friday, I helped her set the dining room table for *Shabbos*. We smoothed out a freshly pressed white linen tablecloth and set out the meat dishes and silverware. Nana checked the Jewish calendar that was thumb-tacked inside the right-hand door of the dairy cupboard to find out what time to *bensch licht* (light candles). The time changed weekly depending on what time the sun was expected to set— in the winter, it could be as early as 4:00p.m.; in the summer, as late as 9:00p.m. Jewish days start at sundown and last until the following sundown. Nana set out her candlesticks on a sterling silver tray. She filled them with candles—all ten of them—on the kitchen table so they would not get in the way during dinner.

"How come you light so many?" I once asked.

Nana's eyes grew misty. "I have two sisters and three brothers. And don't forget about your mother and father."

"But that only makes seven."

"What about Pop and me?"

"That's still only nine people," I insisted. "Who's the last one for?"

She bent over and put her arms around me. "It's for you, my darling," she said, kissing my cheek.

Hugging her as tightly as I could, I did not want to let go.

That day she must have been looking at the clock on the wall above the meat refrigerator because, too soon, I heard her say, "It's almost time for *Shabbos* and I still have to get the stove ready."

Everything had to be finished cooking before Nana *bensched* licht to usher in *Shabbos*. I would watch as she turned off the oven, leaving the meat and potatoes still inside. She turned off the burners on the stove, put a steamy pot of chicken soup followed by one filled with some kind of cooked vegetables on the meat counter, lit the pilot light, put a cookie sheet wrapped in aluminum foil on top of the stove, and then replaced the pots. With the oven turned off, the kitchen still smelled like *Shabbos*. Everything was still hot by the time Pop closed the store and came upstairs. By lunch on Saturday, everything was lukewarm but still tasted good.

I loved standing next to Nana, her head covered with a white silk scarf, as she struck a wooden match and lit the candles, circled her hands around the glowing candles three times as if she were getting ready to give them a hug, and put her hands to her eyes, covering them with her palms. Slightly off key, but with a lot of emotion, she sang the following blessing over the candles in Hebrew:

"Blessed are You, O Lord our God, King of all the world, Who has made us holy through Your commandments, and has commanded us to kindle the light of the Sabbath."

My mother went through the motions of keeping a kosher home. She had two sets of dishes; bought meat from the kosher butcher; and, on the rare occasion that a dairy utensil wound up in the meat sink, she rolled up the sleeves of her shirtwaist dress, pulled her long black-ish-brown hair into a pony tail, and scrubbed the utensil with soap and boiling water.

Our kitchen may have been kosher, but my parents often fed me bacon and eggs for breakfast at the Moose Bar and Grill across the street from my grandparents' sporting goods store or cheeseburgers at the diner for supper.

On a typical Saturday, my mother drove to the Chinese restaurant and brought home supper—usually pork spareribs and pork fried rice. Our basement had an outside entrance, so she could bring non-kosher food into the house without going through the kitchen. As soon as I heard my mother call out my name, I put away the homework I was doing on the kitchen table and looked in the pantry for some paper plates and plastic cutlery. One time, after skipping down the stairs that led to the wood-paneled basement with the built-in bar, I came to a sudden stop at the bottom and started back up the stairs.

"Where do you think you're going?" my father asked, looking at me quizzically through his tortoise-shell framed glasses.

"I forgot to close the kitchen door," I said, with one foot on the bottom step. "I don't want the smell of *treif* (unkosher) food spreading throughout the house."

"Don't worry about it." His clear blue eyes twinkled. "I'm hungry. Let's eat while it's still hot."

I looked over at my mother.

Shrugging her shoulders, she said, "I guess we'll just have to air out the house later."

I helped my mother take the paper cartons out of the big brown paper bag. The succulent aroma of sweet-and-sour spareribs filled the air. My mother placed a large portion of ribs and fried rice on a paper plate. She then proceeded to pick through the rice with a fork, methodically removing all traces of vegetables before handing the plate to my father, who hated vegetables. She served me next, then took some for herself.

We watched the news on the basement televison and silently ate our supper.

On steamy Sunday evenings in the summer, my parents sometimes took me to a small amusement park in the nearby village of Bayville. Having Nana and Pop come along made it extra special. My favorite ride was the boats that went around in a circle. I loved to ring the bell every time I went past the bench where Nana and Pop sat watching me. If I'd been a really good girl that day we'd go to a snack bar—the Pig and Whistle—for ice cream. I could tell we were there by the wooden sign with a colorful picture of a pig painted on it. After my father parked the car, everyone—except Nana, that is—got out and headed for the serving window.

The first time this happened, I walked back to the car and asked, "Nana, don't you want some ice cream?"

"No thank you, darling," she said. "I'm not hungry."

"But the vanilla's so yummy," I pleaded. "I never even let any drip on my clothes."

Leaning back against the seat, and closing her eyes, she told me, "That's wonderful, darling. But I'm not hungry."

By the time I returned to the serving window, my father was almost finished with his cone, which he asked me to hold while he got one for me. The two of us sat down at a wooden picnic table across from my mother and my grandfather who were eating slimy-looking stuff.

"What's that?" I asked, pointing at the paper plates in front of them.

"Clams," my mother said, wiping her mouth on a paper napkin. "Want to try one?"

"Nope," I said, licking my cone, still wondering why Nana stayed in the car.

From my childhood perspective, the Pig and Whistle was no different than the Carvel stand in my hometown. (Carvel is kosher.) Anywhere we went for ice cream was okay with me. But as an adult looking back, I can't help but feel disgusted at my parents' obvious disregard for Nana's attitude toward keeping kosher. *What were they thinking?* Couldn't they have chosen a time when Nana and Pop were not with us to stop at a place with such a blatantly un-kosher name? And then there's the issue of Pop and clams. Did Nana even suspect that he ate them? At this late date, there's no way to know for sure.

Was Pop less religiously observant than Nana? I did not think so at the time. Now that I remember him eating clams, I'm not so sure. No matter, in Pop's retirement he served as *gabbai*, assistant to the rabbi, at the synagogue in my hometown. That honor was bestowed only on someone well versed in the *Talmud* which encompassed, among other texts, the *Torah*—also known as the Five Books of Moses; the *Mishna*—a systematic compilation of the laws of the *Torah*; and the *Gemora*—an analysis and interpretation of the *Mishna*.

I never wanted to upset Nana, but there were some things she was better off not knowing. I did not tell her about the times my parents took me to see the Christmas Spectacular at Radio City Music Hall in New York City, or the Christmas songs we sang together in the car on our way home, or the ornaments I made in art class to decorate the school tree. Or the yummy Christmas cookies our neighbor baked. And I never told Nana how much fun she was missing.

Until rehearsals began for the seventh grade chorus concert, I had no idea that Christmas was anything more than a Christian holiday filled with fun. After the song sheets were handed out for the winter concert, something made me slow down and study each word of the first song: "Away in a manger, no crib for a bed, The little Lord Jesus lay down his sweet head . . ." Despite having sung those words many times before, that was the first time I paid attention to what they meant. The more I read them over, the clearer it became that Christmas was a birthday party for Jesus.

I did not want to drop out of the chorus. But, according to everything I learned from Nana and my teachers at Sunday school, there was only one God. And he was not named Jesus.

I did not know what to do. There was no one to ask. Even my parents sang Christmas songs, so I could not trust them to give me advice. Definitely not Nana—even though I felt closer to her than to my own parents—because I was afraid she would tell me to quit the chorus.

I made my own decision to stay in the chorus, but when it came to singing words like Jesus or virgin, mouthing them was what I chose to do. That worked well. I felt confident that I was not doing anything against my religion. And I did not get into trouble with the music teacher for not singing. The chorus was large enough that she could not possibly hear all our individual voices.

4

ॐ/๑

Worse Than Dead

I used to have a crush on Sammy, our rabbi's oldest son. Of course, I never told him how I felt about him. I never spoke to him at all. I was way too shy. After all, I was only in eighth grade and he was a high school senior. However, since his father was our rabbi, I looked forward to catching a glimpse of Sammy whenever I went to services. But he probably never even noticed me.

It was the first Sunday of summer vacation. My dad was in the backyard grilling hamburgers on the white brick barbeque he had built.

I could hear Greg, my four-year-old brother, shouting "Daddy, let's play catch."

"Not now, son," came the reply, "We'll have time for that after supper."

My mother and I were in the kitchen. She was cutting up iceberg lettuce and tomatoes for a salad and I was making French fries. As usual, I peeled four potatoes, but for variety, sliced them with the crinkle cutter.

When the phone rang, my mother wiped her hands on her apron before answering it. Although I'd expected her to tell whomever was on the line that supper was almost ready and that she would return the call later on, she didn't do that. Instead, she sat down at the kitchen table and listened. Every now and then, I heard her say, "Oh no. Those poor people." Picking up the extension in another room so I could eavesdrop was tempting, but I did not want to take a chance on getting caught. I'm sure the call lasted at least fifteen minutes because, by the time my mother said good-bye, the French fries were done.

As my mother hung up the phone, I noticed her face was flushed. "Are you okay?" I asked.

"We'll talk about it later," she said, not looking at me. She walked into the bathroom, washed her face and regained her composure. What could have happened? Was it something I had done? I could not think of anything. Maybe it was just that someone had died.

Dad and Greg soon took their places at the octagonal wooden kitchen table. Mother and I served supper.

As she sat down across from my father, my mother said, "Something awful has happened! Sammy, the rabbi's son, ran off yesterday and married a Catholic girl!"

I put down my hamburger and stared at my mother. How could he do that to his parents? I was shocked. At that time, in the early 1960's, the rate of intermarriage for Jews in America was less than ten percent. As far as I knew, none of those people lived in my hometown. I wondered why Sammy needed to punish and scandalize his family in such a manner. How could he turn his back on his religion? Weren't there plenty of Jewish girls, including me, who would have married him?

I did not hear anything else that was said until my father slammed his fist on the table and said, angrily, "I'd kill him if he were my kid."

"I think you're overreacting," my mother said, meekly.

A long moment later, my father said, "He's gone out and embarrassed his father. How can the rabbi ever again deliver sermons on ethical Jewish behavior when this is the way his own family behaves?"

"We do the best we know how when it comes to bringing up kids," said my mother. "There's never a guarantee they'll turn out the way we want."

"I expect better than this from my children," my father said.

"I know that," I said softly, noticing my brother playing with his supper.

"We've got a good girl," my mother said, patting my hand.

"What are the Smolowitzes going to do?" I asked.

Shiva is the traditional period of mourning observed by the immediate family. It's a time when friends and relatives offer their condolences.

"Marrying a *shiksa* means that Sammy is as good as dead," my mother told me. "Starting tomorrow, they'll sit *shiva* for him."

"You mean they're going to act as though he died? What if he changes his mind and gets a divorce?"

"The damage has already been done," my mother said through her tears. "To his family he's gone forever."

That was over forty years ago. His parents did not keep in touch with Sammy. But his siblings did. They even helped him pick up his belongings when their parents were not at home. I learned this from Sammy's youngest brother who just happened to join our local synagogue in upstate New York a few years ago. Sammy is still married. He has three beautiful daughters. What a shame that, when his parents passed away a few years ago, they had never even met their grandchildren.

The decision Sammy's parents made must have been difficult, especially for his mother. As a mother of two grown sons, I can't imagine anything that would cause me to stop loving them, to not want to spend time with them. What the Smolowitzes did was the accepted practice at that time. But they were essentially punishing their son for falling in love.

5

Hot Dogs and Hillel

During the second week of my sophomore year at Albany State, I met a guy named Peter at a picnic sponsored by Hillel, the Jewish group I had joined in the hope of meeting Jewish guys. Between bites of Hebrew National hotdogs, we got acquainted. He was a freshman. His Long Island accent reminded me of home.

"What's your major?" I asked.

"Bio," he said, wiping mustard off his short-sleeved plaid, button-down shirt. "I want to teach."

"Me too. I'm a Spanish major."

Pretending to gag, he said, "Spanish is my worst subject. I almost didn't graduate high school because of it." He swallowed the rest of his hot dog. "This sure beats dorm food."

"Your Mom a good cook?"

He nodded.

"Veal parm's her specialty."

"Your house isn't kosher?"

"No. Is yours?"

Shaking my head, I said, "My mother gave up on it when my grandmother stopped eating at our house."

"What happened?"

"She saw my mother use a meat spoon to dump dog food into a dish."

"What's wrong with that?"

"Dog food's not kosher."

We walked over to a picnic table covered with fruit. A sheet of paper was taped on the table.

"You sign up for home hospitality for the High Holidays?" I asked. Nodding, he spit several watermelon pits on the ground. "I'm going to hate being away from home for *Rosh Hashanah* (the New Year)," I continued. "My father's in the choir. My grandfather's a *gabbai*. And I don't want to miss out on spending time with my Nana."

"What'd you do last year?" he asked.

Trying to hold back tears, I said, "The holidays came before school started. This'll be the first time I won't be able to wrap my arms around Nana and wish her *L'Shanah Tova* in person."

"Tell me about your grandmother," Peter suggested. "Maybe that'll make you feel better."

"Maybe later. I'm too upset now. Tell me about yours."

Peter's grandmother worked in a doll factory; his grandfather in a car wash. He told me they weren't the least bit religious.

"Poppy used to take me fishing early on Saturday mornings in Sheepshead Bay," Peter smiled. "Before the boat left the dock, he always managed to polish off both burgers Poppy's Ma had packed for him, and at least one beer."

"Nana and Pop are the most religious people I know," I said, proudly. "But Saturday was the busiest day for selling sporting goods so they had to stay open. Now that they're retired, they spend a quiet *Shabbos* together."

In the distance, someone shouted, "Time to go!"

Sitting next to Peter on the bus on the way back to our college campus, I realized how comfortable I felt with him. Being away from home for the holidays was not going to be so bad after all.

Peter and I wanted to get married right after my graduation, but my parents wanted us to wait until after Peter's, a year later. They offered to pay for my master's degree if we waited, and we took them up on it. Our wedding took place on the Sunday after Peter's graduation.

My brother Greg was only fourteen, but that didn't stop Peter from asking him to be his best man.

I can't help smiling whenever I think about the morning of our wedding.

There I was in front of the bathroom mirror nervously trying to put on eyeliner when something caught my eye. It was Greg dressed in a badly torn undershirt, blue jeans, suspenders, and a straw hat. The rifle in his hands barely made it through the doorway. It was obvious that he was fighting back a smile.

"Going somewhere special?" I asked.

"I heard you're having a shotgun wedding," he said. This was typical of his warped sense of humor.

"You're such a nut!" I said, reaching out to hug him and accidentally tossing my eye liner into the toilet.

Before he could change into his official wedding clothes, I grabbed my Kodak Instamatic and took his picture.

That photo has a place of honor in our wedding album, directly opposite the professional shot of Peter and me signing our *ketubah*.

Peter and I planned on moving back home to Long Island, but the heavy traffic on the Long Island Expressway changed our minds. Instead, we settled in a semi-rural community in upstate New York. Having to pick up our mail at the local feed store seemed so exotic. Who cared that the nearest synagogue was a distance away? We were so naïve! But it didn't take long before we realized that something was missing in our lives. We needed to connect with other young Jewish couples.

Moving was not an option. But we did join a synagogue. After going to services at several of the synagogues in Albany and Schenectady while we were in college, deciding which one to join was not a problem. We joined the smaller Conservative synagogue in Albany because of its size, because we both grew up Conservative Jews (not to be confused with conservative politics) and because I felt that most Reform Jews were too liberal. I assumed the Orthodox were way too religious, though I had yet to enter an Orthodox synagogue.

Sometimes after a long week at work, the thirty-minute drive into Albany either for Friday night or Saturday morning services became tiresome. But there was no other option until someone in our community placed an ad in the local weekly announcing an organizational meeting idea, with the goal of starting our own synagogue.

At least twenty families were represented at the initial meeting. Where had all these Jews been hiding? Almost equally divided between Reform and Conservative with one or two who were Orthodox-leaning, many had moved from the New York metropolitan area. A few from New Jersey; others from Pennsylvania. Several were teachers like Peter and me; some were engineers who worked at General Electric in Schenectady. We came together out of a common desire to be part of a Jewish community. A few were focused on the need for religion in their daily lives. Others wanted to fill the void left by not having family nearby. Although Peter and I were childless at that time, the top priority for many couples was a Jewish education for their children. These parents felt a need to connect with their Jewish background in a formal way, to give their families something that frames the world from a religious perspective.

By the time Congregation Beth Shalom was formalized in 1974, thirty-four families voted to affiliate with the United Synagogue of Conservative Judaism. Our first High Holidays services were held in an unfinished storefront. Over the years we continued to meet in various locations—a local country club, a medical arts building, the reception hall of a church—until 1976 when we decided to construct our own building following the plans for a three-bedroom ranch house with a few modifications.

Peter volunteered to be the first principal of our religious school until there was enough money to hire one. As youth advisor, I did my best to find extra-curricular activities to keep the teenagers interested in Judaism.

Our first religious leader, a retired rabbi and Holocaust survivor, was followed by a succession of part-time rabbis until our congregation was finally able to afford to hire a full-time rabbi. Women's lib had a lot going for it. But I expected the position of rabbi to be filled by a man because that's the way I was raised. Even so, raising my hand to vote at our congregational meeting I came to the conclusion that having a full-time rabbi—even if she was female—was better than having a slew of part-timers with no continuity between them.

Belonging to a synagogue is just that, belonging. The social aspects are just as important to Peter and me as the religious ones. Spending time with friends and acquaintances is one of the main reasons we attend our synagogue. Though I usually enjoy the religious services, there are times when my mind starts to wander and I find myself dozing. When the same thing happens to Peter, I let him sleep unless, of course, he starts to snore. Every now and then, I find myself going out to the foyer to meet a friend for a short chat only to return to my seat refreshed with the bond of peoplehood. Some of our closest friends are those we met at our synagogue. As the joke goes: Eisenstadt goes to synagogue to talk to God and I go to synagogue to talk to Eisenstadt.

I believe that all Jews have a small voice inside of them that says, "I am a Jew." For some, that voice is so weak that they barely hear it. Mine is resolute.

One recent evening when we were out with a group of friends, someone asked me, "Are you a Jew first or an American?"

"A Jew, of course," I said, without hesitation.

Looking surprised, he said, "That makes nine to one."

"I don't understand."

"Out of the ten people I've asked so far, you're the minority. The rest of us are proud Americans."

Was he looking for an argument? I wondered.

"What about the Jews in Germany before the Second World War?" I asked. "Did being German protect them from the concentration camps?"

He had no answer.

6

⚭

Cholent Can Fill You Before It Gets in Your Mouth

At 2:00 p.m. one Saturday toward the end of Yehuda's class in Judaic Studies, he and Chaim wandered into the kitchen looking for breakfast.

"How about brisket?" I suggested.

Slumping down on a chair, Chaim said, "Brisket on *challah*? Great!"

Yehuda stood watching me slice the meat. Though we hugged when he first entered the room, he had yet to say anything beyond a muttered "Good morning."

"Want a sandwich, too?" I asked him

"No thanks," he said. That was a switch. He used to love my brisket sandwiches. "Sorry. Forgot to tell you it's traditional to eat a hot meal on Saturday."

Opening the microwave, I said, "I'll warm it up."

"That's . . . not exactly what I meant."

"What did you mean?"

"I'd like it . . . if . . . you could start making *cholent*." I looked at him. That word sounded vaguely familiar. Had I seen it somewhere in a recipe book? He went on, "It's a kind of stew that cooks overnight so you don't have to cook on *Shabbos*."

"How do you make it?"

He gave that some thought. "Throw beans, meat, potatoes, and, uh . . . vegetables in a crock pot on Friday morning. Saturday afternoon, it's ready to eat."

"Perfect for people with no teeth," said Chaim, showing us his gums.

I once had a crock pot, but regardless of how low I set the temperature, something always stuck to the bottom. No matter how much Peter and I scrubbed the pot, it never came clean. So we threw it out. If buying a crock pot would make Yehuda happy, that was what I planned to do.

I had a vision of myself as a good Jewish cook. Thanks to Nana, traditional Jewish foods were a mainstay of my menu: *hamentashen*, triangular pastry stuffed with fruit, for Purim; *latkes*, potato pancakes, for Chanukah. According to Yehuda, *cholent* is "the cornerstone of a customary *Shabbos* meal on Saturday" just as chicken soup is on Friday night. Why did Nana never make *cholent*? Too bad she was no longer around to ask.

At first I resisted the idea of adding *cholent* to my repertoire. But why miss out on trying another Jewish delicacy? I used to love Nana's *p'cheh*, jellied calves' foot; *schmaltz*, rendered chicken fat; and *grivin*, deep-fried chicken skin.

In the middle of the night a few weeks after Yehuda first mentioned it, the word *cholent* crept into my brain. Where was that recipe? Making my way downstairs in the dark, the slapping of my slippers on the slate floor in the foyer was earsplitting in the stillness. Blinded temporarily by the brightness of the fluorescent ceiling light, I slouched against the kitchen wall, pressing my palms on my eyelids, impatient to begin the search. Some time later, I finally found my four Jewish cookbooks, piled them on the table, and opened the first one, *Cookbook Favorite Recipes from our Best Cooks*, an accumulation of recipes that was once sold as a fundraiser for our synagogue.

On the same page as my recipe for lemon sole was one for *cholent*. The directions were as follows: "Brown thick slices of onion and meat. In a heavy pot place layer of browned onions; sprinkle with flour, salt, pepper and a pinch of ginger. Follow with layer of unsoaked dry lima beans, barley and/or any other dry beans; sprinkle with flour and season. Add meat and surround with cut up raw carrots; several raw eggs in shell may be added. Sprinkle with flour and season. Cover with boiling water and bake in oven at 350 degrees or cook on burner at medium heat for 1/2 hour; turn down to lowest possible heat or place on Salton tray and allow to cook until Saturday lunch." Although it did not say, I guess you were supposed to start cooking this sometime on Friday. The recipe concluded with the following information: "Quantities of ingredients vary with number of people to be served; any inexpensive cut of meat can be used. I suggest stew meat or *calichal*. Meat may be cut into pieces or remain whole. No additional fat need be added."

What a disappointment! How could I ever cook that? With no idea how it was supposed to taste, figuring out how much of each ingredient to use would be impossible. What was the egg for? Why did it have to be in the shell? And what's a *calichal*?

At 3:00 a.m. there was no one to ask. So I went back upstairs to bed.

One *Shabbos*, Yehuda made *cholent* for us. Hard to believe he used to hate to cook. By Saturday morning, the surprisingly sweet yet pungent aroma emanating from the crock pot made it hard for me to wait until lunchtime. When we finally sat down to eat, the *cholent* was delicious. Neither a soup nor a stew, it had a nice chewy texture and a sweet and sour flavor. Chaim also loved it. But Peter definitely did not. He ate only a spoonful or two and, when he thought nobody was looking, dumped the rest back in the pot.

During his junior year at the University of Pennsylvania, Chaim started making *Shabbos* dinner on Friday nights for his friends. His usual fare included chicken with barbeque sauce, a tossed salad, and either a noodle *kugel* or oven-roasted potatoes. His friends took turns bringing some kind of dessert. After dinner, I loved listening to Chaim and his friends sing traditional *Shabbos* songs. At some point Chaim started making his own *cholent,* but he seemed to have a fetish about not cleaning the crock pot until right before he needed it next. So, his apartment always seemed to have a stale and sweet yet pungent odor.

Someone once said, "To die without ever having tasted *cholent* is clearly to have led a wasted life." As the old advertisement says, "You don't have to be Jewish to enjoy Levy's Jewish rye bread." It's also true that just because someone is Jewish does not mean he enjoys *cholent*. Peter does not like most soups or stews so it's not all that surprising that he does not like *cholent*. One of the few soups he loves is Manhattan clam chowder—remember that shellfish is not kosher—and he orders it whenever we eat out. As a matter of fact, before we boarded a plane to Israel to visit Yehuda and his family, Peter accidentally spilled some of his favorite soup on his shirt. No amount of scrubbing was able to remove the telltale red stain. Later on, Peter told me how guilty he felt hugging our son with the remnants of the clam chowder still prominently displayed on his shirt.

7

No Problem With Shorts

It was almost midnight on a Saturday in early April, months after the start of that Judaic studies class. Yehuda was home on break.

Walking past the family room, I heard laughter and realized that he and Chaim were watching television. As I walked into the room, I noticed they were lying side by side on the floor, chins propped up on throw pillows, watching *Saturday Night Live*.

That was a surprise. I had no idea Yehuda still allowed himself to enjoy the bawdy brand of humor emphasized on *Saturday Night Live*, even though it did start at 11:30 p.m., way after *Shabbos* was over. (*Shabbos* traditionally ends one hour after sundown on Saturday.)

"Have fun guys," I yawned. "I'm off to bed."

They returned my hugs and went back to the TV.

"Got to get out early tomorrow if you want to ski," Peter called from upstairs. "Why don't you two get some sleep instead of staying up all night?"

"I know, Dad," Yehuda moaned.

"Takes two hours to get there," Peter said.

"I know, Dad," Chaim grumbled.

"I'm waking you at 5:30."

"We'll be ready on time."

"That'll be the day."

Why did he always have to have that conversation the night before a ski trip?

"Who're they kidding?" Peter asked me a few minutes later. "They're never ready on time."

"Give them a chance," I said. "They might surprise you."

The next morning they were awake way before Peter got to them.

"I need another sandwich," Yehuda said as he helped me make lunch.

Passing him the bowl of tuna, I asked, "Extra hungry today?"

"I can't eat snack bar stuff anymore." He sounded wistful. "They cook bacon."

"Dad loves their cookies. Chaim loves the fries. Not going to ask them to give up those up, are you?"

"Guess not."

Yehuda and Chaim sped off as soon as we reached the top of the ski lift. They flew past us and down the expert slope, showing up at the lodge in time for lunch. No sooner did they take off their jackets and ski hats, then Yehuda mumbled something that sounded like "Whoops" and put his ski hat back on.

"What's with the hat?" Peter asked.

"Forgot my *yarmulke*," came the reply.

"Let's eat already," said Peter, looking annoyed. *What was his problem?*

Peter went for soda. Chaim and I bit into our sandwiches. Yehuda unwrapped his sandwich but did not start eating immediately. I figured he was saying the blessing over bread.

"Hands off my chocolate chip cookies," said Peter, carrying a tray of soda and cookies.

"No problem," Yehuda told him, "I brought an extra sandwich."

"No cookie?" Peter looked puzzled.

"Not kosher," Yehuda said.

"Not my problem," said Peter, taking a big bite of cookie.

Reaching for one myself, I paused to look over at Yehuda and then took a bite.

Our boys slept soundly on the way back home. Even so, Peter and I spoke softly.

"Yehuda seemed to loosen up a little today," I said.

"Talked to him on the lift after lunch," Peter said. "He knows it's not easy for us to accept change. Rabbi Katz told him to take it slow and not expect too much from us at once."

"Things sure have turned around. Our sons used to depend on us to teach them to do things. Now Yehuda's teaching us about our own religion."

"Could still be a phase, like when he was into stamp collecting and then dropped it a few months later."

"He's a lot older now," I said.

"Hard to believe he locked the babysitter out of the house when he was seven."

On moving-out day at the end of Yehuda's freshman year, the last thing Peter and I wanted to do was to visit Rabbi Katz. But Yehuda insisted. And we were curious. So how could we say no?

Pots of pink petunias decorated the front stoop of a two-story brick house. Rabbi Katz, a tall, slightly balding man with a greyish-brown scruffy beard opened the door and greeted us warmly. After watching him hug Yehuda, and shake hands with Peter, I extended my own hand only to have the rabbi put his hand in his pocket, smile, and say to me, "Sorry about that."

This was far from an auspicious beginning to our acquaintance. My lips went dry. There I was trying to greet our son's rabbi in the most polite manner possible only to be insulted by him. That was the first time I'd had anyone refuse to shake my hand. I did not like the way it felt. I was offended, as if my hand was unworthy of being shaken. Back then, I knew nothing about *shomer negiah*, the concept of Jewish law that prohibits touching people of the opposite sex unless they are medical practitioners or specific family members.

This came back to me recently when a friend complained, "Ever since my uncle became Orthodox, he won't hug me any more! What kind of religion stops a man from hugging his niece?"

"The feeling of being rejected must be overwhelming," I said.

"Your sons still hug you, don't they?" she asked.

"Thank goodness. But I once felt snubbed trying to shake hands with an Orthodox man and that feeling of rejection is still fresh."

After listening sympathetically to my tale about meeting Rabbi Katz, she asked, "So you think my uncle still wants to hug me?"

"He'd probably love to, but he's got to stick to his beliefs. The way I understand it, if he bends the rules, the whole thing may fall apart."

As we entered the Katz's sparsely furnished L-shaped living room, the *rebbitzen*, the rabbi's wife, called out from the kitchen to say she would be right with us. It was hot inside and out, but Mrs. Katz was wearing a long-sleeved blouse, a skirt that fell well below her knees, stockings, and pumps. Self-conscious in my sleeveless shirt and shorts, I wondered if we should have come at all. But she did not seem at all bothered by my clothing as she extended her hand and told me what a pleasure it was have to us in her home. Something about the way she said those words made me believe that she really meant them.

"Almost time for dinner," she said. "Why not join us?"

"Maybe another time." I looked at my watch. "We've got a long ride ahead of us."

"At least sit down for a minute and have something cold to drink."

That was hard to turn down.

We were about to sit on the living room couch when I suggested to Peter and Yehuda that we brush off our shorts.

"It's fine," Mrs. Katz said, "With six kids we don't worry about a little *schmutz* (dirt) on the furniture."

Several refreshing glasses of iced tea, and we were back on the road.

"I'm glad you made us stop," I told Yehuda. "The rabbi and his wife aren't the least bit stand-offish."

"I could have told you that," he said.

"But I never met anybody Orthodox before."

"What about me?" he asked.

"Mrs. Katz is pretty easygoing. I would have thought twice before suggesting that three filthy-looking individuals sit down in my living room."

"The only time you let me or Chaim in the living room was to practice the piano."

"The rabbi's jokes are almost as good as mine," said Peter.

Changing the subject, I asked, "The Katzs *really* have six kids?"

"They do," said Yehuda. "I don't understand why anyone would want so many." He had no way of knowing that he and his future wife would have seven children and counting.

Soon after the start of his sophomore year, the Katz's house became Yehuda's second home. Peter didn't mind; but I did. So I decided to take the rabbi up on his offer for our family to spend a *Shabbos* at his home.

"Cool," Yehuda said when he heard the news. "Can't wait for you to see what a traditional *Shabbos* is really like. Dad will love Mrs. Katz's chocolate cake."

When we arrived at the Katz's a few hours before sunset on Friday, Yehuda wasn't there yet. Chaim had a paper due so he stayed home. Mrs. Katz greeted us at the door dressed in what looked like a long-sleeved, ankle-length, black velour evening gown. *Should I have called about the dress code?* Peter had packed a sport jacket, but the only thing in my garment bag was a simple cotton dress.

"I'm so glad you decided to come," Mrs. Katz said, surprising me with a warm hug. "My husband and I were hoping to get to know you better."

After my experience with the rabbi, Peter knew better than to try shaking hands with his wife.

But after giving her the once over, Peter told her, "Don't you look snazzy!"

"Why thank you," she said, sounding surprised. "It's just my *Shabbos* robe. But let's not be so formal. Please call me Shuba."

"We're Peter and BJ."

Following her upstairs, I took the liberty of asking, "What is a *Shabbos* robe?"

I had no idea that my future daughters-in-law would have *Shabbos* robes or that I would, too.

Shuba explained that on Fridays, after rushing to pick up a few last-minute items on her way home from work, cooking dinner, and making sure the kids were ready for *Shabbos*, she was often too tired to get dressed-up.

"That's where my *Shabbos* robe comes in," she said, smoothing down her skirt, "It's comfortable and I can throw it in the wash for next week."

We followed her into a bedroom lined with twin beds. *Twin beds? Haven't slept in one since college.* After she left, we tried pushing the beds together, but they would not budge.

We changed our clothes and then heard Yehuda's voice outside the door.

"Mom? Dad?" he called out. "You up here?"

Even though we had spoken the day before, I still craved his hugs.

Later, in the dining room, Rabbi Katz introduced us to his children. Ranging in age from six to eighteen, they were remarkably poised. Though I offered to help serve dinner, Shuba insisted that I relax. The meal was plentiful and delicious. The conversation was free-flowing. Topics ranged from homework to current events to ideas for upcoming vacations. It was a lot like being at home.

I felt comforted by the realization that Rabbi Katz and Shuba were "normal people" who had interests outside their religion: they enjoyed literature and classical music, read *The New York Times*, and were knowledgeable about current events. Board games and camping were favored family activities. I hadn't expected Orthodox Jews to be so worldly. That weekend helped kindle the warm relationship with the Katz family that continues to this day.

Peter and I ate breakfast alone on Saturday morning. On the kitchen counter, next to a can of instant coffee, a bowl of tea bags, and a pile of paper cups was a hotpot of water and a platter of sliced cake.

Yum. Later we walked to *shul*, the synagogue, with Shuba and her two teenage daughters. The other men, including Yehuda, had already left for morning *minyan*. Orthodox men pray three times a day but are prohibited from reciting certain prayers unless there is a minimum of ten men present. Those ten make up a *minyan*.

Peter found Yehuda up front in the men's section of the synagogue. I sat with Shuba and her daughters in the women's section, in the back. The prayer book contained some English but I still had trouble keeping my place. Some prayers were similar to those at our Conservative synagogue, but the melodies were different. Shuba introduced me to a few friends and neighbors as "Yehuda's mother." I felt like a minor celebrity. It seemed that everyone knew our son. I pretended to be content.

After *Shabbos*, Rabbi Katz turned on the radio in the living room console to catch up on the news. While changing our clothes for the trip home, Peter and I discussed the fact that the Katzes did not seem to have a television.

"Think there's some Orthodox taboo against TV?" Peter asked me.

"TV is something I would hate to have to live without," I said, never expecting that Yehuda would one day ask us to do that very thing.

8

Hard to Study on Skis

Our second Parents Weekend was different. Yehuda insisted we accompany him to services at the Center for Jewish Life not only on Friday night but on Saturday morning, too. As if that was not enough, he made us eat all our meals at the CJL. Peter and I weren't sure what to make of this but decided it would not hurt to go along with whatever Yehuda wanted.

We were getting ready to go home on Sunday when Yehuda suggested stopping at his dorm on the way to our car. Knowing the traffic would be heavy if we didn't leave soon, we were tempted to turn him down. That is, until the look on his face showed me that something was bothering him.

"What's wrong?" I asked.

"Nothing," he said, shrugging his shoulders. "Tell you when we get to my room." He is so much like me that I knew better than to try pushing for details before he was ready to talk.

Yehuda sat down on the edge of his bed and looked down at the floor. Peter smoothed out the rumpled sheets and plopped down next to him. Fighting the urge to comment on the clothes scattered at the foot of the un-made bed, I searched for a comfortable place to stand.

Eyes still downcast, Yehuda said softly, "I found a new place for winter break."

"Tired of skiing with your old dad?" Peter joked.

"Of course not," said Yehuda. "But I don't want to go skiing."

It took a second for me to process this. He used to love skiing so much that in high school he worked as a ski instructor at Gore Mountain, forty-five minutes from our home.

"What do you want to do?" I asked.

Looking up at me, he said, "I want to study . . . at a *yeshiva* . . . in Israel." A *yeshiva* is an institution dedicated to the study of Jewish texts.

I could not believe what I was hearing. In college, studying was the last thing I wanted to do during vacation.

"You'd rather study than ski?" Peter asked, standing and turning to face our son.

Yehuda nodded.

"Why Israel?"

Yehuda seemed so happy to talk about it that his dimples started to show.

"There's this great *yeshiva* in Jerusalem called Ohr Somaach. Rabbi Katz said it's the best place for a *ba'al teshuvah* like me who did not grow up Orthodox."

"Why wait till now to tell us?"

"Didn't want to spoil the weekend."

"Can't you go some other time?"

"I really want this!"

Though impressed by his dedication to Judaic learning, I was not ready to let him go just yet.

"We'll get back to you on this," I said.

His arms around me, he said, "I knew you'd understand."

In the mid-1990s, there was a relative truce in that part of the world, so I wasn't worried about Yehuda's safety. Though I did not want him so far away, he was nineteen, old enough to make a lot of his own decisions. And it was important to let him grow up. Pressuring him to ski with us when there was another place he would rather be was not playing fair. Why try to prevent him from learning more about our religion? Hard to believe he was the same kid who once refused to join Hillel. And after that fraternity turned him down, he never tried another. Maybe Orthodox Judaism served the same purpose for him.

Seeing Yehuda off at the airport was painful, but before starting down the runway, he came back to us for a few more hugs. Maybe it was my imagination but he seemed to hug more tightly than ever before. I somehow survived the next six weeks. He promised to call home often, but the seven-hour time difference made that difficult. I hated missing his calls. Hearing messages on our answering machine—about the friends he made and the historic sites he visited—made me miss him even more.

Yehuda's trip to Israel had a stronger impact on our family than I imagined. Though I hoped that his learning about Judaism was just a whim, who knew he would someday make a career out of it? Or that within six months Chaim would want to go to Israel?

Chaim had his own journey to Orthodox Judaism. No telling how much it had to do with Yehuda's change, but the route Chaim took was just as arduous. At sixteen, no amount of cajoling could convince him to stay with the youth groups at our synagogue; he was tired of the same Jewish kids. Israeli dancing at an Orthodox synagogue in Albany, thirty minutes away, was what he wanted. But neither Peter nor I would drive him. We encouraged him to have Jewish friends but weren't willing to go out of our way to help.

Not long after he returned from Israel, Yehuda called to tell us he was ready to go back.

"Winter break again, next year?" asked Peter.

"The whole year," Yehuda said.

"But you were just there," I said, trying not to plead. "And we've hardly seen you."

"Mom, don't try to lay a guilt trip on me!"

"What's that again?" Peter sounded distracted. He must have been watching TV.

"Yehuda wants to go back to Israel for an entire year," I said, as calmly as I could.

"How could you do this to your mother?"

"Call it junior year abroad."

"Same *yeshiva* as before?"

"Why not?"

I found myself wondering how things would have turned out if we had not let him go to Israel that first time. Would he still have wanted to spend an entire year there? And why didn't I want him to go back? Maybe I was afraid of missing him too much. That wasn't like me to be so selfish. After all, what mattered more, his happiness or mine? And what about the summers I spent studying in France and Spain once our sons were old enough for summer camp? Having experienced the beauty of studying the language and culture of a country up close, how could I turn him down?

In the midst of deciding whether Yehuda should go back to Israel for a year, Chaim tried to convince us to let him go there on a Jewish teen tour that summer. Was it a coincidence that the trip Chaim wanted to go on was sponsored by Camp Ramah, the camp that made Yehuda take that Judaic studies class?

This was the summer before Chaim's senior year of high school, so he would still be home with us for one more year. He was only seventeen. There would be plenty of chaperones on the trip. I wanted him to have Jewish friends. He wanted to go to Israel. A Jewish teen tour might be the solution.

Chaim signed up for an optional excursion to see first-hand what it was like to be in the Israeli army. Conditions in Israel were still fairly peaceful, but I did not want him to do anything dangerous and hoped he would not go through with it. Even so, he called us one day from an army security post.

"You'll never guess where I am," Chaim said, sounding secretive.

"Riding a camel?" I asked.

"That was days ago. Now I'm on guard duty."

"On what?" I asked, hoping I misheard.

"Guarding the girls' dorms?" Peter joked.

"Just finished basic training," Chaim said. "Now I'm somewhere in Gaza at an army outpost. But I'm not allowed to tell you where."

I did not like the sound of that. Playing army seemed fun for him. To me, it was serious business. Peter and I had lost friends in the

Vietnam war. This was a little before the start of the first Arab Intifada. I hated that Chaim was in Gaza, but the tour director had assured me before they left that the teens would only go to places that were considered safe.

"How's it going?" Peter asked, not sounding the least bit concerned.

"Slept in the barracks." Chaim sounded excited. "Fired an M-16 at target practice. Gotta go. Looks like some Arabs are trying to pass through."

I waited nervously for him to come back home.

Chaim came back fired up about Israel. He brought us a picture of himself in an army uniform holding two M-16's. To my surprise, he was more religious than when he left. Instead of wearing a *yarmulke* only when he went to synagogue, he started wearing one all the time, explaining to anyone who asked that wearing a *yarmulke* was his way of showing his pride in being a Jew. Chaim also started getting up a lot earlier so that he would have time to *daven*, pray, before starting the rest of his day.

9

Defensively Offensive

As Yehuda's religiosity increased, so did my mother's criticism. I soon developed the habit of holding the phone away from my ear and letting her rant that I did not call or visit her enough, was not sympathetic enough about her ailments, and refused to be at her "beck and call" the way she had been with Nana. Chaim was undergoing his own religious transformation, but that completely passed her by. When she started in about Yehuda—but never to his face—I told her he had the right to make decisions about how he lived his life. Still not sure how I felt about his new religious bent, I found myself in the position of defending it. The more belligerent my mother became, the harder I defended Yehuda's right to be religiously observant. The more defensive I became, the more I believed my own words.

To my mother's way of thinking, Nana, my long-deceased grandmother, was the foremost authority on things Jewish. That Nana had been Conservative—not Orthodox like Yehuda—should have made a difference to my mother, but it did not.

The following phone conversation was typical:

"Why is his hair so short?" my mother asked, without mentioning Yehuda by name. "Pop's wasn't."

Instead of reminding her that my grandfather was bald, I simply said, "His choice."

Orthodox men wear a small prayer shawl under their shirts that has four corners with *tzitzis*, fringes, tied to them. These fringes sometimes hang below the shirts.

"What's he trying to prove by wearing *tzitzis*? Pop never did."

"Yehuda's Orthodox," I said. "Pop wasn't."

She let that pass.

"His shirts are always wrinkled. Is that some strange religious rule?"

"Probably doesn't care."

"Why doesn't he celebrate Thanksgiving? Nana did."

Having already asked that question myself, I was able to reply, "He told me we should be thankful for every day. No need to set aside a special day."

"Fine," she said, sounding annoyed. "He has a perfectly good *English* name. Why Yehuda all of a sudden?"

"He likes it," I said, impatiently. "Doesn't that make you happy?"

"Should it?" She sounded surprised.

"His Hebrew name came from Pop," I reminded her.

"How can you let him waste his life?"

Unable to take any more I said, "Ask him yourself."

The tone of her interrogations has lessened a bit, but every now and then she still finds some way to get my goat. For example, upon learning that Penina was pregnant with their sixth child, my mother called me to ask, "When do you think he's going to stop trying to prove his virility?"

10

The Cranberry Bogs of Israel

Yehuda left for Israel in early August, intent on spending all his time studying *Torah* at the *yeshiva*, but Princeton put a damper on that. To receive credit for the year in Israel, he had to take some courses at an accredited university—in this case, Hebrew University. Bummed by this, he had no idea that he would one day be grateful for the Yiddish he learned at Hebrew U.

He would be home for Passover in six months, but that was too far off for Peter and me. Peter's new job selling computers allowed him to take time off. Unfortunately, my teaching job did not. However, after a lot of wrangling, promises, and paperwork, the school district decided to let me take off one week without pay to visit Yehuda. Having spent the previous summer in Israel, Chaim, a high school senior, was eager to return. Taking time off from school didn't faze him at all.

Yehuda sounded excited about our visit, but not about the hotel we reserved for our stay.

"The travel agent said it's kosher," we told him. "We can eat Thanksgiving dinner there."

"Kosher enough for the travel agent," Yehuda said. "But I heard the kitchen is not well-supervised, they cook on *Shabbos*, and there's no *Shabbos* elevator." A *Shabbos* elevator automatically stops on every floor.

It seems that pushing a button is considered a form of work prohibited on *Shabbos*.

I hardly slept during flight. It felt great to hug Yehuda when he met us at the airport looking tan, healthy, and happy to see us. Following him to a waiting taxi, I got my first glimpse of Israel—high-pitched horns honking, people pushing and shouting words in a language I did not understand. The air smelled of fried meat, onions, and peppers. After watching the driver strap our luggage on the roof of the taxi, I climbed in and found myself next to a woman with a crying infant on her lap.

As Yehuda settled into the seat next to me, I whispered, "Who are *they?*"

"Don't know," he whispered back. "Thought you and Dad would be happy to save a little money," he said proudly. "This is a shared taxi. The more stops we make, the less it costs."

I kept my opinion to myself.

As we slowed down in front of a hotel, Yehuda said something to the driver and we sped off again.

"You sound good in Hebrew." I said.

"Thanks. I've learned a lot."

Thinking back to my childhood, I adored the two afternoons a week in Hebrew school and looked forward to more, only to be told that two years of Hebrew was sufficient for a girl. Looking out the window of our taxi, I wondered why it was so easy for me to follow the Hebrew in prayer books but impossible to read the words on the street signs we passed. I was puzzled until Yehuda pointed out that Israelis leave off vowels when they write.

I was yet to find out that Israel is not an extension of the United States; it is an independent country with its own language and customs. Israelis do not celebrate Thanksgiving and they rarely, if ever, eat turkey. Thank goodness we packed cans of cranberry sauce.

It was still quite warm in Israel at the end of November. I was comfortable on *Shabbos* wearing a cotton blouse and skirt. Peter and Chaim looked well put together in their tan pants, light blue shirts, and dark blue sport jackets. But Yehuda, in a black suit and white shirt, blended in with many of the other people on the street. I tried not to stare at the Hassidic Jews, dressed the way their ancestors did in the old country, in long black belted jackets, short black pants that barely reached below their knees, and long white socks. How did they manage with those heavy-looking fur hats?

"Are we near the Wailing Wall?" Peter asked, interrupting my train of thought.

"The *Kotel*?" Yehuda asked. "We'll go there after lunch."

"Lunch sounds good," I said, realizing how hungry I was. "What's that word you used?"

"*Kotel*," Chaim chimed in. "That's Hebrew for 'The Wall.'"

"Good job!" Yehuda said, patting his brother on the back. "How'd you know that?"

"I was here last summer."

The *Kotel* was once the western supporting wall for the second Temple. Over the past thousand or so years, so many Jews visited that sacred site to cry over the destruction of the Temple that it came to be known as the Wailing Wall. After years of Arab control, it was reclaimed by the Jews during the Six Day War in 1967.

Walking across the plaza toward the Wall, I felt humble. My fingers tingled. What a wonderful place for the four of us to pray together!

All of a sudden, I heard Yehuda say, "See you later, Mom."

"Where are you going?" I asked, surprised.

"The men's side, of course."

"See ya," Chaim smiled.

"Sorry," said Peter.

How could I have forgotten that religiously observant men and women don't pray together? Watching the three of them walk away, I felt like a lost little girl. In the midst of hundreds of other women praying, I was alone. Everyone else seemed to know what to do, what prayers to say, when to bow, and where to stand. Embarrassed by my ignorance, I felt my face flush. The woman next to me, in a drab green suit, smiled and offered me her prayer book. Smiling weakly, I put out my hand and then noticed the tiny print was all in Hebrew.

It was pretty quiet on the women's side, just the sound of murmured prayers. But there was singing coming from the men's side.

Why weren't the women singing too? Later on, Yehuda explained that Orthodox men are forbidden to hear a woman singing, unless she is part of their immediate family.

Forcing myself to act grown-up, I held back tears. Walking closer to the Wall, I reached out over the heads of the women in front of me. The stony-looking surface was surprisingly smooth. As I kissed the tips of my fingertips that had touched the Wall, I started to cry. I wiped my eyes, but the tears kept coming. If someone hadn't motioned me to move out of her way, I would never have moved from that spot.

Pastrami Does Not Grow on Trees

Yehuda was so content in Israel that I expected an argument when summer came and it was time for him to leave. But that didn't happen. Even better, he sounded eager to start working at a Wall Street firm, in New York City, less than three hours from home. His new job developing a web-site for the human resources department involved using knowledge he had gained in his computer science classes at college. Peter and I hoped he would enjoy the job so much that he would give up on *yeshiva* learning and come back to the reality of the working world.

A single room in a dorm at Columbia that came with access to a small kitchen where he could cook with his own kosher pots seemed a perfect place for him to live, at least at first. But the realities of life in a co-ed dorm made him extremely uncomfortable. So before the end of the week, he moved into an apartment on West End Avenue that belonged to Rabbi Katz's friend, who was spending the summer out of town.

We wanted Yehuda home with us on weekends but he refused to ride on *Shabbos*, our synagogue was too long a walk, and our Conservative services no longer met his needs. So we drove to New York City on Sundays and spent the day there with him. Too bad Chaim couldn't be with us. He was working at a sleep-away camp.

There were so many kosher places to eat in the city. Yehuda picked dairy for lunch and meat for dinner. In accordance with the dietary laws, he waited six hours after a meat meal before eating dairy. Dairy is easier to digest so there is no long wait before eating meat after a dairy meal. At Nana's, if we had brisket for lunch, we didn't have cheese blintzes until right before bedtime. So maybe Yehuda was right after all.

A few weeks into his new job, we went to a deli for dinner. Peter and I were stuffing ourselves with coleslaw, sour pickles, and corned beef when I noticed that Yehuda was slouching in his seat and staring at the ceiling.

"Not hungry?" I asked.

Eyeing his uneaten sandwich, Yehuda moaned, "That job is so annoying. I knew I'd hate it."

"Why'd you take it in the first place?" Peter asked.

"Didn't want to disappoint you."

"Just put up with it till college starts."

"Princeton said I could spend next semester back in Israel."

When did all this happen?

"Don't we get to vote?" Peter's voice rose in volume with every word. "This job was supposed to bring you down to earth."

Trying to keep from screaming, I said, "There is a world *outside* the *yeshiva!*"

"I'm old enough to know what I want!" said Yehuda.

People seated nearby were staring.

"Shh," I said, index finger to my lips. "We're causing a commotion."

"Hard to believe Princeton is okay with this," Peter said, his voice a little softer.

"Unlike Princeton, the *yeshiva* forces me to use my brain."

Sipping some water, I tried to soothe my nerves. With his mind already made up, what we would accomplish by arguing? We had done our best to give him a good background. It wasn't up to us to decide what was important to him; it was up to him.

Yehuda returned to Israel for the beginning of his senior year, but only after agreeing to return to Princeton for his final semester. Before long, he changed his mind and decided to stay in Israel for the foreseeable future. A degree in computer science was worthless, he insisted.

What he would learn at the *yeshiva* was invaluable. If we shipped him his textbooks, he offered to read them if he had time. *How dare he?* We had never gone down that road before. And I didn't like it one bit! We would not let him drop out of college so close to graduation. He was old enough to make his own decisions. But not this one! We were disappointed and also angry. We thought about threatening to cut off his tuition. But that wouldn't bring him home or even back to Princeton. We were stumped.

Ever since that first *Shabbos* with the Katzes, Peter and I had kept in touch with them every few months. So, at that difficult time in our lives, we turned to them for advice.

A few days later, the rabbi told us, "Yehuda will honor his original commitment or I'll go there and drag him back."

Peter and I were overjoyed when Yehuda returned to the States for his final semester. No longer comfortable with the distractions of a secular dorm, he found a room in the dorm of a small *yeshiva* not far from the college campus.

"I don't fit in," he insisted. "I'm a stranger, the only observant Jew on campus. I barely go to class."

Yehuda graduated with honors but, after a celebratory dinner at the CJL, informed us that he was going back to Israel. His words caught me by surprise. Having looked forward to his graduation, I hadn't given much thought to anything else.

That evening, while Yehuda learned *Torah* and Chaim watched TV, Peter and I sat on the edge of our bed.

"Is he ever going to give up this learning stuff?" Peter asked me. I had no answer. "Israel is a waste of time! And if we let him go, how do we know he'll ever come back?"

Sadly shrugging my shoulders, I said, "In his mind, he's already there."

"Let's get the rabbi's take," Peter said, picking up the phone.

"Yehuda will be better off in Israel," was Rabbi Katz's advice. "Give him time to decide what he wants to do with the rest of his life. If you pressure him to stay in the States, you may not be happy with the results."

The Mir Yeshiva in Jerusalem turned out to be the right choice for Yehuda, but not for me. Two years later I was still asking when he was coming home to stay.

In the Guise of a Matchmaker

Rabbi Katz's older son and daughter were in Israel during one of our visits there with Yehuda, so we invited them to dinner. Judging by their black hats, black pants, black sport jackets, and white dress shirts opened at the collar, Yehuda and the rabbi's son and could have been brothers, especially compared with Peter's green chinos and green checkered shirt. By coincidence, the rabbi's daughter and I both wore navy skirts. Her blouse was pastel pink, mine hot pink. If I had known then the Orthodox attitude toward wearing bright colors, I might have worn a different blouse. Then again, maybe not.

Friends had asked me about arranged marriages in the Orthodox world and I had not known what to tell them. Asking Yehuda was out; I didn't want him to feel pressured to get married. So I saved the topic for an opportune moment. Dinner that night was the moment.

While waiting for dessert to be served, I asked the rabbi's eighteen-year-old daughter, "What's the story with arranged marriages?"

"What do you want to know?" she asked.

"This guy will probably get married at some point," I said, placing my arm around Yehuda. "I'd like to know what he's in for."

Yehuda groaned.

"The whole thing's quite simple," said the rabbi's son, in a serious tone. "The *shadchen*, the matchmaker, takes two big pots and fills them with the names of the eligible guys and girls. When a guy calls, she closes her eyes and pulls out the name of the girl he's destined to marry. If a girl calls, she pulls out a guy's name."

That sounded absurd. But I thought he was telling the truth.

Turning back to the rabbi's daughter, who was directly across from me, I asked, "Really?"

She nodded silently. But a second later, she started laughing, as did her brother.

"What's going on?" I asked.

"They're pulling your leg." Yehuda grinned.

Sometimes, I'm so gullible!

"Sorry," the rabbi's son told me.

"Me too," said his sister. "Here's how it really works. Before the *shadchen* sets you up with anyone, she has to know the type of person you want to meet."

"Looks and personality?" asked Peter

"Yes," she nodded. "But there's a lot more. Would you want to date a guy who plans on moving to Australia? Or the only boy in the family who's accustomed to being waited on? We're told to look beyond the exterior. But a short guy probably wouldn't want to marry someone taller than he is."

Tempted to ask the rabbi's daughter what type of guy she was looking for, I decided to keep my mouth shut.

Inside and Outside the Freezer

The phone in our bedroom rang early one Sunday morning. Peter answered it before I could open my eyes.

Nudging me, Peter said, "Yehuda's getting married!"

"Who is she?" I mumbled into the phone on my side of the bed.

"All I said was I'm ready to get married," Yehuda told me. "I'm almost 24. Just need to meet the right American girl."

"You're coming back?" I practically shouted into the phone.

"I knew you'd like that."

"When?"

"Soon."

"Where will you live?" I asked, daring to hope that he'd be living at home.

"Beacon, New Jersey. They've got a great *yeshiva*."

I should have expected that.

Things were not tense in Israel, but it was still comforting to have him home, even if only for a few days before he started at the *yeshiva* in Beacon. Having told us he'd bought a black hat in Israel, he had yet to model it for us. So when he dashed upstairs before dinner on his last night home, we figured it was to show off his hat, a fedora. While he was gone, Peter donned his black molded plastic ski helmet and I put on the black plastic cowboy hat I'd purchased for the occasion. Yehuda returned a few minutes later, a wide-brimmed black felt dress hat displayed on his head. Despite wishing him *Mazel Tov* on his purchase, I did not like the hat at all. He looked like a character in a history book, not my son.

As soon as he noticed what was on our heads, he laughed and then hugged us.

"Nice of you to go out of your way to make me feel comfortable," he said. Then, looking pensive, he went on, "The guy's father usually does it." *Does what?* "But Dad, would you mind if Rabbi Katz acts as my intermediary once I start dating?"

"Can't make a date on your own?" Peter asked.

"You're taking the fun out of dating," I said.

"Before I agree to meet a girl, someone's got to check up on her parents, her religious upbringing, her educational background, her goals, and her future plans. Marriage is the ultimate goal of dating. I don't want to waste time with anyone who doesn't match my qualifications.

"You make it sound like some kind of research project," I said.

"What kind of qualifications?" Peter asked.

"Dating is always serious business. I want to marry a college graduate who grew up in a religious home and wants her husband to continue learning for a few years before he enters the job market. And her family has to be honest in their business dealings."

Looking incredulous, Peter asked, "Did I really hear you say the word job?"

The conversation continued after dinner.

Confused by Yehuda's comment that the *yeshiva* forced new students to stay "in the freezer" for six months, I said, "I assume you don't mean that literally."

"There's a six-month waiting period before we can date."

"Sounds crazy to me." Peter said.

"Why would they care if you went out?" I asked. "Besides, how would they know? They don't hire private detectives, do they?"

"Dating's supposed to be such a distraction that once you start, you have trouble concentrating on anything else."

I could not believe he was going to put up with all this. Was he really the same person who sneaked out of the house to go to co-ed drinking parties when he was in high school?

Peter asked a question that was on my mind. "When you're out of hibernation, does the *yeshiva* throw a big party and invite all the eligible girls?"

Yehuda kept silent but I sensed his impatience. Pretty soon, he told us about one of his friends who insisted on only going out with girls who were both beautiful and at least 5'4" in height. Two years later, he was still searching for his physical ideal.

"That's not going to be me," Yehuda said.

In high school and college, Yehuda had enjoyed the friendship of girls but never had any girlfriends. He told us that the first date was always a blind date.

The point of each date, which would take place in public areas, such as a hotel lobby or a museum, was to allow the couple to become acquainted with each other. After each date, Rabbi Katz would talk to both Yehuda and the girl to verify whether or not they would like to meet again. If one of them did not, the rabbi would break the news.

"I'm sure that as time goes on and you get to know her, you'll want to take her to a place where the two of you can be alone," Peter said.

"No way, Dad!" said Yehuda. "It's not like that. Since I've become more religious, I would not even hold a girl's hand until after we're married."

Maybe this type of restrictive dating could work, I thought. The couple could learn about sex together once they were married.

I winked at my husband. When we were dating, Peter and I had gone beyond holding hands. If you liked someone, how could you keep from touching each other?

Yehuda told us about friends of his who went out with more than twenty girls before they met their future brides. But he expected to meet his perfect mate right away.

14

෨෦

No Freezer Burn

Six months after his Beacon Hills *yeshiva* classes began, Yehuda told us that Rabbi Katz had a girl for him to meet.

"Our kosher butcher also has a girl he would like you to meet," I said, truthfully.

"Tell him 'thanks,' but I'm busy right now," Yehuda said.

"You'll never know what you missed," joked Peter.

"Spent a lot of time at Rabbi Katz's brother's house in Israel," Yehuda explained. "His wife runs a girls seminary, but she's also a *shadchen*. Wanted me to meet one of her former students who was back in Israel for a few weeks."

"Don't leave us hanging," Peter said. "Go on with your story."

"That was a few weeks before I was due to come back to the States. So even though that girl sounded really cool, I told the *shadchen* I didn't want to take a chance on getting involved with someone and then having to break it off to come back home."

"Why bring this up now?" I asked.

"Rabbi Katz's sister-in-law has been pestering him, bringing up that same girl, and insisting that she is 'really special.' She's so positive we'll be perfect together that she's been calling Rabbi Katz from Israel a couple times a week just to make sure I agree to go out with her. I owe it to the rabbi to get this woman off his back."

Yehuda felt he was taking a chance by agreeing to meet this "really special girl" who was already twenty-five but still single. Most of his friends had married girls barely out of their teens.

Yehuda seemed tense when he came home from *yeshiva* for spring break, a few days before his first date with this new girl. He was nervous about meeting her. His good suit needed to be taken in. The brightly colored shirts he used to wear, but had asked me to give away, were still hanging in his closet. I kept hoping he would some day want to wear them again.

"What if she's perfect and I don't make a good impression?" he asked us.

We tried to convince him that she would be the lucky one, but he seemed intent on being nervous. In an effort to help him lighten up, one morning we wore our black ski helmets and our bathrobes to breakfast. It felt good to see his face open up into a smile as he told us how ridiculous we looked.

He was in a much better mood when he left for Brooklyn and his date with that "really special girl." We loaned him a cell phone so he could let us know if he decided to sleep at a friend's house instead of driving the four hours back home later at night.

Yehuda called us the next day.

"I can't wait to see her again," he said. "She's so wonderful. I'm pretty sure she's interested in me. At least, I hope so."

"That's neat," I said, trying to control my excitement. Maybe this background checking really did work. "What's her name? What does she look like? Does she have a heavy Brooklyn accent? What do her parents do?"

"Cool it," Yehuda said. "I just met her. Her name's Penina, but I don't remember her last name."

"Where'd you take her?"

"Sat in the lobby of the Marriott Hotel for five hours. Don't know where the time went. When they started sweeping the floor, I took her home."

I had always kept travel journals, so I bought a new notebook to keep track of the courtship. From the little Yehuda shared with me after his first date with Penina, this experience was more important than any trip I had ever taken.

It was hard to keep from asking about Penina, especially since he refused to tell us about her. Initially he went out with her just once a week, so traveling from our house to hers—with the car we loaned him for the occasion—staying overnight with a friend, and returning home the next day did not present a problem. This was during a break from the *yeshiva*. Although Yehuda had promised to help me prepare for the upcoming holiday of Passover—which involved buying special groceries, cleaning out cupboards, lugging up boxes of Passover cookware and dishes—after his third date with Penina, he decided to stay full-time with his friend instead of coming home between dates. His excuse was that he didn't want to put too many extra miles on the car, but I knew he wanted the flexibility of being able to see Penina on a whim without the prior planning involved if he stayed at home. Whenever I mentioned her name, he sounded happily distracted. He finally told us that she had dark hair and spoke with a Brooklyn accent.

"You sound so exhausted after each date," I told him. "You said that dating involves just sitting and talking. I believe you. But something's going on you're not sharing with us."

"You promised to respect my privacy."

"Are you sure you two aren't getting into a little hanky-panky?" Peter asked.

"How could you even ask? All we do is talk."

"Must be some heavy-duty talking," I said.

Orthodox dating does not usually go on indefinitely. The couple needs to decide within a few dates whether or not their personalities mesh. To have a successful marriage, it is important that they share common values.

From the meager details Yehuda gave us, we knew that each date with Penina was better than the previous one. He was so impressed when he lost his way driving back to her house and she didn't point out his mistake.

I later learned that Penina's parents were frustrated by her being "so selective" in finding her Mr. Right. They had hoped she would have been married by the time she turned twenty-one. Undaunted, she had compiled a long list of questions to ask prospective suitors and was willing to wait until she met someone who had all the right answers.

Penina's questions dealt with moral, philosophical, and religious issues. While our son wanted to "win her over," he wanted to be honest in his responses, which meant forcing himself to do some serious thinking and not merely socializing. He needed her so badly, he told us, that this was the "most exhausting challenge" he had ever faced. That's why he was always tired after a date.

The suspense was impossible for me to bear. Yehuda was in love with someone I had never met. Was she as wonderful as he imagined? Would I like her? What did she look like? What kind of clothes did she wear? When would I finally meet her?

"I told her that you respect my religious beliefs," Yehuda told us. "But she needs to hear it directly from you. And she wants you to meet her parents."

I did not want to come across as overeager, but I couldn't wait.

"Set it up and we'll be there," I said.

Despite my friends' misgivings toward the Orthodox—which they freely shared with me as soon as they learned of Yehuda's religious bent—I was not swayed. Even so, during the course of his religious transformation, he and I had had our moments. At some point, I realized that every argument about his Orthodox beliefs was probably pushing him further away. He was happy with his life in the Orthodox world. If I wanted to keep up a connection with him, I had to start accepting more and arguing less. So when Chaim told me that the Orthodox services at college were more meaningful for him than the Conservative ones at home, I was far more receptive than when Yehuda had told me the same thing three years before. I had come to realize that there are far worse things than having Orthodox sons.

Though I had no qualms about Yehuda marrying an Orthodox girl, what difference would it have made if I had? He needed someone right for him, not for me. My parents had not particularly liked Peter, but that hadn't stopped me from marrying him.

What to wear for meeting Penina and her parents for the first time? Yehuda told me what not to wear.

"Pants for men only. Nothing red, too showy. No short skirts, no plunging necklines, no short sleeves. Dress modestly."

My favorite color was red. My wardrobe consisted mainly of pants, short skirts, short sleeves, and plunging necklines. Some of my winter dresses might have been okay, but it was April. The temperature was already in the 60s. Suits seemed too businesslike. But a short-sleeved navy blue dress did pass Yehuda's scrutiny when I put a pink jacket over it.

Our meeting place was the Holiday Inn in Monsey, a halfway point for both families. Yehuda was so nervous he didn't stop talking the entire drive.

"Her Dad might come off as standoffish," he told us. "Give him a chance. He'll warm up."

"You talk to him a lot?" I asked.

"Says hello, tells his wife to get Penina, and says 'bye when we walk out the door."

"Think he's shy?" I asked.

"Can't tell. I don't stay long enough."

"Her mom's nice?"

"A real homebody. You'll like her."

"I love hermits," Peter said. "She ever go outside?"

"She's quiet. But she always offers me something to eat."

"A good cook?" I asked.

"Don't know."

When Yehuda started reminding us about the no handshaking or hugging rules, I told him not to worry.

"Her mom's younger than you," he went on. "No grey hair."

"At all?" I asked.

"She wears a *sheitel*."

"Could be some grey hidden underneath," I said. "Why a *sheitel*?"

"Wife's hair should only be seen by her husband."

"Anything else we need to know?" Peter asked.

"Relax and be yourselves."

Arriving a few minutes early gave me a chance to comb my hair. I was not nervous. I just wanted to look nice. I wanted to show my best side. I had no preconceived notion of what to expect, but I was eager to meet Penina and her parents. Surely they must be special people if they raised the girl Yehuda wanted to marry. This felt like I was interviewing for a new job: mother of the groom. Peter was concerned that we would have nothing to talk about. Yehuda was so tense that he stood in one spot staring at the floor until they arrived.

Shloime, Penina's father, had a long beard and was dressed in a black suit, a white shirt and a black fedora, like Yehuda's. Peter wore a navy blue sport jacket, black pants and a pale blue shirt. And he had remembered to put on a *yarmulke*.

Penina had auburn hair and a sensational smile. She and Malka, her mother, had on navy blue suits. Remembering what Yehuda had said about a *sheitel*, I tried not to stare at Malka's head. Her hair was medium brown, but I couldn't find any sign that it was not her real hair.

As we sat facing each other, I noticed Yehuda and Penina exchange a fleeting smile, avert their eyes, and then continue sitting silently on the edge of their seats.

We parents monopolized the conversation. When Shloime asked where we live, I started to explain that we live north of Albany, the capital of the state, but Peter interrupted me.

"Do you know how Albany got its name?" he asked Shloime.

"No," answered Shloime.

"Well," Peter chuckled. "When Henry Hudson and his son Ben were sailing on the Hudson River, they could not go any farther. When they started to turn around, Ben asked, 'Is this the end?' 'Yes,' his father told him, 'That's all Benny.'"

Who would have thought that a corny joke would be the thread that tied our two families together? No sooner did Peter deliver the punch line than I began to groan, and, much to my surprise, Penina and her parents started to laugh.

Next, it was Shloime's turn.

"You just reminded me of how Staten Island got its name," he said to Peter. "The same Henry Hudson and his son were on their way back to New York City when Ben pointed to something in the distance. 'Dad, that an island?' Ben asked. 'That's right, son,' Henry said. 'Staten Island.'"

It was hard to miss the groans coming from Penina and her mother, but I hadn't heard that one before so I laughed right along with my husband. This was the first indication that, although we came from different backgrounds, Peter and I had much in common with Penina's parents.

"Where do you work?" Peter asked Shloime.

"I'm a chemist at a pharmaceutical company," said Shloime. "We test new drugs for toxicity." It surprised me to learn that his co-workers were not Jewish. This told me he was aware of and might be accepting of the secular world, which included Peter and me.

I talked about my recent retirement from teaching. Peter gave them a brief run down of his work history, explaining that he had once taught eighth-grade science, had taken time off for an MBA, went on to work with computers, and now ran several convenience stores and car washes.

I wondered if Malka was overwhelmed by meeting us, her daughter's potential in-laws, because she spoke only in response to questions posed to her. She was a bookkeeper at a jewelry firm in New York City. She smiled broadly when explaining that she never worked on Thursdays because that was when she babysat her granddaughters. She and Shloime have three other children, a younger son and daughter, and an older son whose wedding had taken place five years before.

Just the opposite of what Yehuda had told us, Shloime's personality reminded me of Peter's; they both loved telling corny jokes. Although Peter omitted all off-color jokes from his repertoire that day, he and Shloime did keep each other on a roll. And Malka and I commiserated over our husbands' shared sense of humor. After she mentioned that

Penina was a National Merit Scholarship winner and had a masters degree from Brooklyn College, I told her that Yehuda had graduated with honors from an Ivy League college.

"We're proud of Yehuda's religious commitment," I said, to get everyone's attention.

Once the topic was raised, Penina's parents wanted to know about Peter's and my religious background. I told them we were both brought up as Conservative Jews, but my grandmother had been very religious. Maybe being devout had merely skipped a few generations, I suggested.

Yehuda and Penina sat so still while we parents got acquainted that I almost forgot they were with us. Suddenly, three hours had passed and it was time to leave. Malka, Shloime, Peter, and I agreed we had enjoyed ourselves so much that we hoped to meet again.

But the final decision was up to Penina.

After the others left, Peter and I walked Yehuda to the parking lot. We were going home. He was going back to his friend's house. Although it was tempting to ask his impression of the meeting, the look on his face told me he wanted to be left to his own thoughts. I assumed he was thinking about whether or not he would see Penina again.

But the very next day he called during his eighth date with her.

The first words he said when I answered the phone were, "*Mazel Tov*, Mom and Dad." That meant he and Penina would be getting married!

My mouth went dry and a barely audible, "*Mazel Tov*," squeaked out. After a few gulps of cold water, I screamed, "*Mazel Tov!*"

"Thanks," said Yehuda, sounding mellow. "Penina wants to talk to you."

"*Mazel Tov*," I said again, not quite shouting.

"Thanks so very much," Penina said. "I knew Yehuda and I were meant for each other. And after meeting you and his dad, I'm positive. You're so supportive of his religious beliefs!"

"We're proud of him," I said. "After all, we're all Jewish."

"Is it okay if I call you Mom? That's what Yehuda calls you."

"I'd love it!" I said, feeling privileged by her request. So many friends had told me their daughters-in-law never called them anything. I tried to calm down, but it was hard.

Chaim was finishing up his senior year at college. Though I'd kept him up to date concerning his brother's courtship of Penina, he probably knew more about it than I did. Yehuda and Chaim had become much closer once Chaim returned from his first trip to Israel wearing a *yarmulke*.

According to Penina, she and Yehuda had eaten dinner at a fancy restaurant in New York City and were now on their way New Jersey to tell Rabbi Katz the good news in person.

"Next, we'll go to my house," she said. "My parents will invite my aunts, uncles, and cousins over for a *l'chayim*, a toast, in our honor."

Malka and Shloime called us an hour later saying they wished we could be there to celebrate with them. It felt great to have them share our excitement and happiness.

"Since today's Tuesday, the *vort* will probably be next Monday," Malka said. "We'll let you know as soon as it's set."

"What's a *vort*?" Peter asked.

"Like an engagement party," Shloime said. "The kids will exchange words of commitment. *Vort* means 'word' in Yiddish." Peter and I hadn't had an engagement party because my mother convinced me it was just a way of asking for gifts. Since it had a Yiddish name, I hoped a *vort* was something different.

15

FLOP Means a Lot

When I asked Malka about helping with the *vort*, she said that she and Shloime would take care of everything. This was a switch from what I had heard about engagement party horrors that included disputes over who would pay for the party and who would be invited. Those wounds could last for years. I'd even heard about an engagement party that was sponsored by the bride's parents and included only five invitations for the groom's side.

Although I was thrilled when Malka suggested inviting anyone we wanted, it was doubtful that many of our friends and relatives would be able to come on a weeknight.

Peter and I wanted to do the right thing, but were unsure whether we should offer to pay for the *vort*, so we asked Rabbi Katz.

"The bride's family always plans and pays for the *vort*," the rabbi told us.

"What about the wedding?" I asked.

"That's a different story," he said. "The groom's parents are usually responsible for FLOP."

"What's that?" Peter asked. "Sounds like a disaster waiting to happen."

"Flowers, liquor, orchestra, and photographer," the rabbi said and then cautioned me to let the fathers discuss expenses because the mothers traditionally planned "the meal, the flowers, and so on."

Though unhappy with this automatic division of responsibility, there was nothing I could do about it.

Hoping to get something special for Penina, I asked Rabbi Katz's wife for suggestions.

"Silver candlesticks are a customary gift to a future daughter-in-law," she said. "That way she'll be able to light candles to welcome *Shabbos*."

"I'd love to bring them with me to the *vort*, but I don't know what she would like," I said.

"Take her shopping. Brooklyn has some great stores."

"I love to shop. And that'll give me a chance to get to know my future daughter-in-law."

On Friday morning, Penina called to wish us a "Good *Shabbos*," her voice sounding as if she had been crying.

"Are you okay?" I asked, concerned.

"Yehuda sent me a bouquet of flowers," she sighed. "They're so beautiful."

"So why are you crying?"

"I sent flowers to my friends when they got engaged, but I never realized how much that gesture can mean, especially from Yehuda."

The day of the *vort*—about two weeks after Yehuda proposed— I woke up early, too excited to sleep. Yehuda had reminded me that Orthodox women never wore pants, especially no jeans, so I put on a skirt and blouse. It felt strange dressing that way for the car ride to Brooklyn, but as I was entering the Orthodox world, I wanted to follow their traditions. This was part of my evolution, the art of self-adaption. I started turning into a chameleon right after Yehuda asked Penina to marry him. Over time I have found my own way of living my life while still having Orthodox children and grandchildren.

Malka and Shloime had reserved a room for us in Midwood Suites. The dark furniture and heavy décor reminded me of my grandmother's apartment when I was a child. I felt at home. On the nightstand stood a framed picture of Yehuda and Penina along with a hand-written note that said, "Welcome Mom and Dad."

Choosing this hotel, as compared to an impersonal hotel chain, was typical of Malka and Shloime's thoughtfulness. The more contact we had with them—we spoke to them at least once a day—the more obvious it became that our mutual goal was our children's happiness.

Shloime and Malka had suggested meeting at their house to discuss wedding plans before we went to the *vort*. As Shloime opened the door, Malka held out her arms. So I hugged her, happily.

Sitting with them at their dining room table felt comfortable, like being with old friends. Malka set out some delectable-looking cookies, and we'd purchased an assortment of fancy nuts and chocolates, but we spent a lot more time talking than eating.

In spite of FLOP, Shloime was overwhelmed by Peter's offer to pay for half of all the expenses.

"Are you sure you want to do that?" Shloime asked. "If all your friends and ours come, we could have four hundred fifty guests."

"Don't worry about it," said Peter, casually.

I gulped audibly but said nothing, remembering Rabbi Katz's warning to leave the monetary matters to the men.

When Peter mentioned that we planned to charter a bus to transport our guests to the wedding, Shloime insisted on paying for half of that expense. In between telling corny jokes, the two fathers were perfect examples of cooperation.

"We found two halls for the wedding," Malka told me. "One's more elegant and costs a bit more. We put a hold on both till you see them."

Choking back tears of happiness, I said, "You raised a great daughter. The choice of halls is yours. We trust your judgment." I knew this sounded syrupy but I really meant it.

The wedding plans progressed smoothly. We agreed on everything: the band, catering hall, flowers, with no desire to impress each other. The word "elaborate" was not in our vocabulary. After Malka showed me the Hebrew-only invitation from their older son's wedding, I asked her to include an English translation with Yehuda and Penina's.

Since we would probably be too busy to eat at the *vort*, we had an early dinner at a nearby kosher restaurant. Penina joined us, but Yehuda had warned us he might skip dinner and nap in the car. After a full day at the *yeshiva*, he expected to be exhausted. But he showed up at the restaurant anyway. This was the first time I saw him since he and Penina became engaged. It was fantastic to be able to hug him and see how euphoric he was about marrying Penina.

There was a special electrical charge in the air as soon as Yehuda's eyes met Penina's. Facing each other at opposite ends of the table they barely spoke and just picked at their food.

Malka suggested arriving at the hall a little early.

Taking my hand, Penina said, "Mom, don't worry. I'll show you the ropes."

Shloime and Malka led us through separate entrances to the ballroom where the *vort* was to be held. A cream-colored, six-foot-high, opaque linen screen, otherwise known as a *mechitza*, divided the rectangular room. If Peter and I were on different sides of the room, who would I talk to if I became bored?

Malka must have read my mind.

"Everyone's looking forward to meeting you," she told me. "Once the guests arrive, you'll be so busy you won't even miss the men."

As clothing styles changed over the years, so had the clothes I wore to work. Though the suits from my early years of teaching were replaced by a collection of pants and tops, a few skirts and blouses lingered in my closet, coming out whenever I felt the need to look professional. As the clothes worn by my fellow teachers gradually deteriorated to jeans and T-shirts, my most casual attire in the workplace was a denim skirt.

During the course of Yehuda's budding religiosity, I had worn whatever I wanted. But the black and cream ensemble I wore for the *vort* was too covered-up for my taste; it seemed like a disguise. That the pin-wale pleats of the floor-length skirt made me look almost pencil thin, only added to the subterfuge. At least the pearl-drop earings I'd worn to my own wedding represented the real me.

I had no choice but to remain on the women's side of the *mechitza*. Inhaling deeply in an attempt to relax, the perfume of a tropical rain forest filled my lungs. I took in the magnificent floral displays on the tables that ran the length of the dividing screen. In addition to long-stemmed and tea roses in red, pink, white, and yellow, as well as purple lilies and white orchids, there were several exotic varieties I had never seen before, each accompanied by notes wishing "*Mazel Tov*" to the happy couple.

Interspersed among the flowers were chocolate tortes, seven-layer vanilla cakes, seven-layer chocolate cakes, carrot cakes, Linzer tortes, cheese cakes, and over twenty varieties of exquisitely decorated cookies. Dominating this display was a three-foot high glass jar filled with huge chocolate-chip cookies.

"What's the story with these?" I asked Malka.

"A gift from Penina's friends," she explained. "Ever since she was little, she baked chocolate chip cookies to help her friends celebrate *simchas*, special occasions. This is their way of thanking her."

We were standing by the door when Penina floated into the room, looking dreamy. She and Yehuda had driven together so they would have some time alone.

"It's a good thing you got here," Malka said, checking her watch. "The guests will be here soon."

Holding up her wrist to display an exquisite diamond bracelet, Penina said, "Yehuda just gave me this. Isn't it gorgeous!" Turning toward me, she added, "I'm grateful to you for bringing Yehuda up to be so thoughtful that I . . ."

She was interrupted by the sound of women calling her name. As Penina introduced me to her family and friends, each one shook my hand, smiling widely, and telling me how happy she was to meet me. Many told me how wonderful Penina was and how special Yehuda must be if she agreed to become his wife. Despite being treated like an honored guest, I couldn't help feeling self-conscious. What if all those faces, crowned with stylishly coiffed *sheitels* recognized me as an impostor but kept it to themselves out of respect for Penina and her family?

I continued standing next to Penina until I heard a familiar female voice. Amidst the sea of Penina's family and friends, I barely recognized my college roommate in her hat and covered-up clothing. I wanted to chat with her, but there was no time. Penina's friends and family kept arriving and they each wanted my attention.

Penina soon took my hand and introduced me to six of her closest friends. In her honor, they had done something "highly unusual." Instead of spending a customary evening at home with their husbands and children, they had driven two hours to the *vort*, leaving their husbands in charge of their children.

Later that evening, Rabbi Katz appeared on the women's side and asked Penina, Malka and me to join him on the men's side for the *tenaim*, to hear him read the certificates of betrothal. I did not understand any of the Hebrew that Rabbi Katz read. Malka treated me to a simultaneous English translation.

Before returning to the women's side, she and I were handed a dinner plate wrapped in a cloth napkin.

"What's the plate for?" I asked.

"We're going to break it," Malka explained. "A broken plate is impossible to put back together in a perfect fashion. Together, you and I will break this plate to show that the bond between our families is impossible to separate.

"What a beautiful tradition!" I said, teary-eyed.

"This ceremony is often postponed until right before the wedding so the couple has time to back out if things don't go well between them."

"But our kids are perfect together!"

"That's why we're not waiting to do this."

After Malka and I broke the plate against the back of a metal chair, Peter, Yehuda, and Chaim held me in their arms.

Soon Shloime walked over to us.

"A hearty *Mazel Tov*," he said, hugging my husband and sons. "Consider yourself hugged," he added, smiling at me.

The *vort* was a wonderful whirlwind experience, no time to be bored or to miss the men. I must have smiled a lot because my cheeks hurt.

As Peter and I helped Malka and Shloime load the flower arrangements and some other gifts into their car, Peter asked, "What do you do with all these?"

"Store the gifts at our house until the wedding," Shloime said. "We'll drop off the flowers at local nursing homes and hospitals, so others can share in our happiness."

"All of them?" I asked.

"Penina wants to keep the ones from Yehuda and dry them," said Malka.

"Good morning, Mom and Dad," Penina said when she met us for breakfast the next day.

"Consider yourself hugged," Peter said. "That was my kind of party. Great desserts, no real food, but great company." There was probably hard liquor on the men's side of the room, but Peter's not a heavy drinker.

"It was fantastic!" I said. "Everyone went out of their way to make us feel welcome."

Peter and I had met too many people to remember all their names, so Penina tried to help out by describing her favorite relatives.

"We have such a large family that sometimes my mom has to remind me how some are related," she admitted.

We lingered over breakfast, chatting until the waitress reminded us that others were waiting for our table.

Peter went back to the hotel.

Penina and I had a date to shop for candlesticks. Strolling past a hat store, my future daughter-in-law said, "I wonder if they sell *snoods*. I'm going to need at least one after we're married."

"What's a *snood*?" I asked.

"Come with me," she gestured. "I'll show you."

Entering the store, I noticed the back wall was covered with what appeared to be small cloth sacks in various shades of black, grey, blue, white, pink, and beige.

Penina tried on a black one that covered her hair and hung down the back of her neck.

"What do you think, Mom?"

What was I supposed to say? If Penina were my daughter—instead of my future daughter-in-law—I might have told her the truth that wearing a *snood* did absolutely nothing for her. But I was out of my realm, dealing with a different culture, a different mode of dress. In an effort to be tactful, I suggested trying on a few others for comparison.

We giggled as she tried on various colors and styles. I didn't tell her that they all looked like overgrown fabric shower caps. In the end, we agreed that the first one was the best.

As we worked our way toward the silver shops, she warned me that picking out candlesticks might take a while. Indeed, the selection was overwhelming. There were at least fifty to choose from in the first shop and Penina inspected them all. I was careful not to comment until after she had a chance to pass judgment on a few, in case she liked a design that looked garish to me.

Gesturing toward an elaborate three-foot-high candelabrum, Penina whispered, "The curlicues on that one would look better on top of a cake."

"We might find a recipe for those," I joked. "Would you like them better in chocolate or strawberry?"

"My mother says I drive her crazy."

Malka had warned me that her daughter was "very picky" and "hard to please," but shopping with Penina was just like being with my girlfriends.

"I'm having a great time!" I said, in earnest, not wanting the adventure to end.

The candlesticks she chose, many stores later, were engraved with an elegant floral design, exactly what I would have picked for myself.

As we left with our purchase, my future daughter-in-law hugged me tightly and invited me to come *sheitel* shopping with her and her mother after lunch.

"Why did you bother with *snoods* if you're going to wear a *sheitel?*"

She seemed delighted to answer my questions.

"I'll wear the *snood* around the house, especially when I wash my *sheitel*."

"Remind me why you've got to cover your hair after you're married."

"It's a form of modesty," she said, patiently. "Certain areas of a woman's body are meant to be seen only by her husband."

"If a *sheitel* makes a woman look more glamorous, how is she being modest?"

"No matter how attractive it might be, a *sheitel* doesn't have the same allure as the woman's real hair. By the way, a *sheitel* is not kosher unless someone who knows *sheitels* can tell whether or not you're wearing one."

"I thought only food was kosher."

"There are guidelines for *sheitels*."

There was so much I wanted to know.

"Some women wore hats to the *vort*," I said. "Think they had *sheitels* on underneath?"

"Might seem like overkill, but some people think they look better in hats."

When she said that some Orthodox women shave their heads, I started to worry.

Yehuda would not ask her to do that, would he?

"You're not talking about yourself, are you?" I asked.

To my relief, she shook her head.

"But you'll keep your hair covered, even at home?"

"If someone comes to the door, I won't have to look for cover."

"We're not just going to a *sheitel macher*, a wig maker," Malka told me during lunch. "We're going to a specialist. Her work is so in demand that we were lucky to get an appointment."

Parking in front of a private home, Malka walked to the side entrance. After she rang the doorbell, a buzzer sounded, unlocking the door, and Penina and I followed her into the basement where the air was thick with the strong scent of hairspray, and conversation was difficult over the loud whirring of hair dryers.

My eyes stung. I started sneezing. Once my vision cleared, I saw blond, brunette, dark brown, black, and auburn *sheitels* displayed on shelves behind the sales counter. A few were long and straight. Some had ponytails or headbands. Others were beautifully coiffed in the latest styles. Each wig sat on a Styrofoam form that gave it a ghost-like quality. I never knew such a place existed. Too bad my camera was back in the hotel. This would be hard to describe to my friends.

We were escorted to the fitting room, where the specialist asked Penina to sit in a beauty parlor chair in front of a mirror and then told her, "First, I'll measure your head and then we'll talk about your new color and style."

With that, she pinned up Penina's hair and placed a thick, mesh-like net shaped like a bathing cap over it. Penina's ears stood out. She looked ridiculous.

"This will be the base of the *sheitel*," the stylist went on. "I'll tug at it and pin until it's a perfect fit. You'll have a chance to pick a new look. What color would you prefer?"

"I don't want to change my natural color," Penina told her.

"In that case, I'll take a few snips to catch all the variations. You'll never miss a few snips."

"Go ahead," Penina said, softly.

"How about style and length? Want a new hairdo?"

"I'd like to keep the same length and style."

"Sounds good to me. You have beautiful hair."

"Thank you."

"I'll take a Polaroid to remind me to sculpt the *sheitel* in the right style."

I was fascinated. The entire procedure took about fifteen minutes, during which the three of us barely spoke.

The *sheitel* would be ready for a fitting in six weeks. Penina could pick it up a few days before the wedding.

Rabbi Katz's wife had informed me that the future mother-in-law usually paid for the *sheitel*. I was not going to break with tradition. However, never having bought one, I tried not to choke when I heard the price was over one thousand dollars.

"This is the expensive one," Malka told me. "I feel bad having you spend so much. Next week, we'll buy another. I'm sure that one will cost less. I'd be happy to pay for this one. If you want, you can get the other."

"Thanks for the offer," I said, "But it's okay." How often did I have the privilege of buying my daughter-in-law's first *sheitel*? On the way out of the shop, I asked, "Why two *sheitels*?"

"One for weekdays; one for special occasions," Malka explained. "Some women even have more."

❧❧

16

Hard to Keep From Passing Out in the Heat

My mother's reluctance to accept Yehuda's religious beliefs did not seem to affect her generosity. Upon learning that he was going to propose, she presented him with her own one-carat diamond ring to use as an engagement ring.

The ring was too large for Penina so I was afforded another opportunity to spend time enjoying her company. Malka recommended a jeweler in the diamond district but begged off when I suggested she join us.

"I really hate shopping," she told me. "Besides, I don't want to spoil your fun."

When I told my friends about going to the diamond district, one told me, "You just have to know how to deal with the vendors. They begin with sky high prices, but with persistence you can get a bargain."

"This is one time I don't intend to economize." I said firmly.

"If you don't play the game, you'll pay too much and miss the fun."

I barely slept the night before and almost forgot to bring my mother's ring. The train ride seemed a lot longer than the usual three and a half hours. The temperature was in the mid-seventies. I was sweating in a long dress and jacket. *How do Orthodox women keep from passing out in the heat of a hot summer?* I brought along a dressy black straw hat to cover my head in case we had time for lunch. I had no intention of making Penina uncomfortable by not covering my head while I ate.

Penina was as beautiful as I remembered. She was dressed in a navy blue suit and tights! As soon as she saw me, she rushed over to give me a big hug. It was fantastic to hear her say, "Mom, I was really looking forward to today. It was such fun last time we were together."

This may sound like a love-fest but I was enthralled with Penina. She made Yehuda happy, which was great by me. Her Brooklyn accent took me a while to get accustomed to. Other than that, she was perfect. I enjoyed her company. Not only was she sweet, sincere, polite, and well brought up, she was in love with Yehuda and wanted to know all about him. She had no idea he had a black belt in karate or that he was an expert skier.

"Isn't that the kind of stuff you talk about on dates?" I asked.

Shaking her head, she told me that she had been dating for a long time. By the time she met Yehuda, she had compiled a mental list of questions that needed answers before she agreed to continue beyond the first date.

"Questions?" I asked.

"About the guy's goals. How he planned to support his family. How many children he wanted to have. One guy was really sweet, but after he told me he planned on having my parents support him, I knew he was not for me."

What kind of idiot would assume that she and her parents would go along with that?

"No wonder you dropped him," I said. "Getting back to your list of questions, what about hobbies?"

"What a guy enjoys doing before he has a family isn't as important to me as the way he plans to lead his life afterwards."

Before long we found our way to the correct booth at the diamond exchange. After examining my mother's diamond, the jeweler brought out ten trays—each one displaying at least fifty different settings. It would have taken me hours to make a selection, but Penina knew what she wanted. Within a half-hour she found it, a simple, elegant white gold setting.

When she picked out a wedding band, I suggested she get a matching one for Yehuda. Peter wears one. So do all my friends' husbands.

"Jewelry is something women enjoy," she explained. "A watch is functional. Orthodox men don't wear anything but a watch."

The jeweler directed us to a booth where an expert would place the diamond in the setting. Next we were ushered to a different locale for the rings to be polished.

"Come back in one hour," the girl behind the counter said quickly.

"Can't we wait here?" I asked, concerned about leaving the rings. How could I be sure they wouldn't substitute a different stone for my mother's diamond?

"Mom, they must do this all the time. I'm sure the jeweler's reputation rests on the fact that he can be trusted."

"I guess you're right. How about a snack while we wait? It must be close to lunch time."

We ordered tea and fruit salad at a kosher luncheonette and sat down to relax.

"This is so marvelous, Mom. My friends will be jealous when I tell them how much fun I'm having with my future mother-in-law. They're always happy to share tales of mother-in-law mayhem."

"Everyone's got some of those," I groaned.

I was about to repeat one of Peter's numerous mother-in-law jokes when I realized there was something far more important I needed to say. My heart pounding, I told Penina how uncomfortable I felt around my own mother-in-law; how she needed to be in control; that we did not get along; and that this had started way back when Peter and I were dating.

Sitting up stiffly, I said, "I want to tell you that I'll do my best to stay out of your hair." At that point I had no clear plan in mind.

Taking my hand in hers, Penina said, "Mom, you don't have to worry. You're terrific!"

As corny as those words might have sounded if someone else had said them, I could tell that she meant every one.

Gently squeezing her hand, I thanked her and wiped my eyes.

Penina was a reading specialist at an elementary school in Brooklyn. I used to teach remedial reading. We had a lot in common.

"I really love challenges like the dyslexic kids who've experienced so much failure that they've almost given up hope of learning how to read," she told me.

"I've heard they're a handful in a group situation," I said.

"I give them the individual attention they need. That's why they progress so quickly with me." Just then, the waiter brought our check. "Will you let this snack be my treat since you seem to be paying for everything else?"

"Thanks a million."

It was Friday. She had to get home early for *Shabbos*. I had expected to pay at least $500 just for the setting of the diamond, but the entire price of the wedding band, the engagement ring, and the cleaning totaled less than $200!

The following weekend, Yehuda came home. I was delighted. It was hard to remember the last time we'd had him to ourselves. After dinner, Peter escorted him into the family room for a "man-to-man" discussion. As I was placing plastic wrap over the leftover brisket, I heard my husband say, "Now that you're going to be a married man, don't you think it's time to give up this *learning* stuff?" Wondering about the same thing, I leaned into the room.

"I'm learning *Torah*," Yehuda said. He sounded annoyed.

"When are you going to go out and get a job?" was Peter's next question.

"Penina and I agreed that these are my learning years."

"What are you going to live on?"

"She's got a full-time job so she can support us for a while."

"How long is a 'while'?"

"I don't know."

Silence.

I walked into the room and sat down between them on the couch, but neither Yehuda, sitting stiffly at one end, nor Peter, arms tightly crossed on his chest, seemed to notice.

Trying to ease the tension, I leaned over to Yehuda, kissed him on the cheek and told him how good it was to have him home.

Turning toward me, his deep brown eyes looked sad. "At least someone's happy."

"Sorry you're so upset," I said. "But what's so important about whatever you're learning?"

"How can you not understand?" he stammered. "The *Torah* has been the lifeline of the Jewish people for generations."

"So?" Peter asked.

Yehuda stood up, glaring at us. "I should have known you weren't really interested."

"But we are," I insisted.

Yawning loudly, Peter looked at his watch and announced, "It's getting late. Any idea where you're going to live?"

"Near the *yeshiva* in Beacon Hills so we won't need another car."

"You're going to make Penina travel an hour and a half to her job in Brooklyn?" Peter asked.

On his way out of the room, Yehuda said, "Unless she finds a job in Beacon."

Accepting Yehuda as an adult who could make his own decisions was more difficult than accepting his religious beliefs.

"Remember what it was like when we thought we were adults and our parents tried to give us advice?" I asked Peter.

"This is different," he said.

"How?"

"Now we're the parents."

Yehuda spent most of the weekend in his room.

17

Double Framed

A few days after Mother's Day, I got a phone call from Penina.

"Did your Mother's Day gift arrive yet?" she asked.

"For me?" I asked, surprised.

Yehuda or Chaim sometimes sent me a card and Peter often bought me roses a few days afterwards, insisting that the florists jacked up the prices right before Mother's Day.

"Of course for you," Penina said. "I mailed it over a week ago so it would get there on time."

"I'm sure it'll show up," I said, "Thanks for thinking of me."

We went on to share our excitement about the wedding. In my mind, I kept coming back to how different it was going to be for me to have another woman in my immediate family.

The next day a small rectangular package in brown paper arrived with the word fragile stamped on it. On the top line of the address, in Penina's elegant handwriting, was the word "Mom." It usually takes me a while to open a package but, in this case, I ripped it open, impatient to find out what was inside. Wrapped in layers of white tissue paper was a black enamel picture frame that unfolded to reveal two photographs that were taken next to the flower arrangement Peter and I had sent to the *vort*. From my perspective, those flowers were unremarkable when compared with the ones that other people had sent. No matter, Penina told us they were the most gorgeous flowers she had ever seen. I seem to recall that they were displayed toward the end of a long table.

When someone asked to take our picture, Penina insisted on posing next to our floral arrangement.

There I am, standing next to Penina. Wide-brimmed black felt hat, chin-length dark brown hair. This was before I decided to have my hair streaked with blond and cut really short. I am in the black and white floral two-piece floor-length ensemble that felt like a disguise. Penina is hatless. As a single woman, she did not have to cover her head. Her hair is light brown with natural blond highlights. She is wearing a navy blue silk suit with shiny silver buttons and a shiny silver belt buckle.

We're both smiling. Penina looks absolutely ecstatic.

In the other photo, my arm is around Yehuda's shoulder. His black hat makes him look so tall. I remember him telling me he had bought the black suit, white shirt, and navy silk tie especially for the *vort*. The beginnings of a beard are visible—more than just a few hairs, a deep dark brown covers his chin.

Both of us are smiling, but Yehuda looks euphoric.

Painted across the top of both photos are the words, "To Mom, With Love."

I called Penina to thank her.

"I'm glad you like it," she said. "Some people like fancier frames."

"It's absolutely perfect," I replied.

Next I called Yehuda.

"What gift?" he asked.

I should have known better.

It's been a while since Penina sent me those photos, but they're the first things I see when I sit down to write at my desk.

It may sound corny but having Penina as my daughter-in-law is enough of a gift.

18

Why Waste a Good Gown?

A friend and I were in a bagel shop when she asked me, "What're you wearing to Yehuda's wedding?"

"Penina offered to shop with me in Brooklyn," I said. "But if I buy a gown there, I'll have to schlep it home on the train and find someone to do alterations."

"What's her mom wearing?"

"The same gown she wore to her son's wedding five years ago."

"You've got to be kidding!" My friend waved her arms, spilling coffee on her lap. "How could she be so rude to her daughter? Isn't she afraid someone will recognize it and think she's too cheap to buy a new dress?"

I was shocked by my friend's outburst, but I helped her mop up the coffee.

"Just because you and I might not do that does not make Malka cheap," I said firmly. "She'd rather spend money on more important things."

"I didn't mean to insult anyone. What's the dress like?"

"Gold and black."

My favorite gowns were the red ones I wore to my sons' *bar mitzvahs*. Neither one covered enough of my body to be considered modest. The wedding was scheduled for the first week of July. In early May I started dress hunting, with the hope that an appropriate outfit would be easy to find. What a disappointment! All the gowns in the stores were too low-cut, too short, or too ugly. One suit would have been perfect, but the beaded jacket left an indentation on the back of my neck.

My friends warned me that bridal shops catered only to the rich, but I was willing to pay whatever was necessary. My heart pounded as I told the bridal shop saleslady what I was looking for. Not only did she tell me it was the wrong season for long sleeves and high necklines, she added that it would take at least a month to special order such a gown. The wedding was less than two months away. I was desperate. When she noticed my quivering lower lip and the tears dripping down my cheeks, the saleslady handed me some tissues and a drink of water and offered to check the back room a little more carefully.

I couldn't help hugging her when she came back holding a gown.

Rushing into the dressing room, I changed out of my jeans and T-shirt and slowly lifted my head to look at the gown. It was a magnificent shade of royal blue. Though sleeveless, it came with a long-sleeved jacket. I tried not to breathe as I stepped into the dress and put the jacket over it.

I felt regal as I looked at my reflection in the mirror. This was exactly what I was looking for. It needed only minor alterations and was only slightly over my budget.

Once I got home, I phoned Penina. My sons never got excited about their clothes, so it was wonderful to have her to share this with.

But before I could tell her about my success, she jumped in with, "Mom, I have marvelous news! My wedding gown is just gorgeous! The top has a plain jewel neckline, long sleeves, and a high waist. The skirt has two pleats that open up into yards and yards of fabric. Pearls and beads are sewn in a floral design on the cuffs and the skirt. It's perfect and it won't take them long to sew the new bodice."

"New bodice?" I asked. "What about the top you just told me about? They sell the gown in two pieces?"

"The gown I tried on is sleeveless and has a plunging scoop neck. A lot of the stores in Brooklyn cater to both the religious and the secular crowds. They often order extra fabric along with each gown, in case they need it for alterations."

"Your gown sounds exquisite. I pictured it in my mind as you were describing it."

We chatted for the next hour, but I did not mention my gown; it could wait.

19

My Seat if You Please

During the wedding reception for one of Rabbi Katz's children, there was a different person in my seat every time I came back to the table. I didn't know if this was typical of Orthodox weddings, but it sure was annoying to have to ask the intruders to give back my seat. And when they finally got up, they acted as if they were doing me a favor. Didn't they have their own places to sit at other tables? Years later, I learned that in the Orthodox world inviting more people than there are seats is fairly common, similar to the airlines overbooking a flight. Some people say that they plan to come, but don't show up. Others say they can't make it but show up anyway.

"I'm sure that won't be a problem with our friends," Peter told me as we counted the number of tables to tell the caterer to set up for Yehuda's wedding. "But when it comes to Yehuda's *yeshiva* friends, we'll probably need an extra table. According to him, you never know until the last minute exactly who has the time to take away from *Torah* study in order to show up."

We had already sent out the following letter to our friends:

> As you know, Yehuda and Penina are getting married on Sunday, July 1, 2001 in Brooklyn. We decided to send you some information to make your planning easier. We will be sending out invitations as soon as they are printed.

Time - The wedding will start about 6:30 p.m. and end about midnight.

Travel - We plan to have a bus from Clifton Park to the wedding. The bus will return to Clifton Park after the wedding. We will get you the details when they are set. The bus will also stop in Albany to pick up our Albany friends.

Parking - If you are driving, there will be valet parking.

Appropriate dress for an Orthodox wedding - Since the wedding is a religious event, it is customary to dress modestly. For men, a dark color suit is appropriate. For women, a suit or dress that covers the collarbone, elbows and knees is appropriate. Women do NOT wear slacks to a wedding. Also, bright red clothes are not usually worn to a wedding.

Physical Contact - There is a law in Judaism prohibiting physical contact between men and women. In keeping with this law, Yehuda will not shake hands or hug any women, and Penina will not hug or shake hands with any men.

We look forward to sharing this wonderful experience with you. Please call us if you have any questions. We are learning as we move toward the wedding and want to share this information with all our friends. We want everyone to be comfortable and have a GREAT time!

Fondly, BJ and Peter

A week later, we sent out the following guide that Penina and Yehuda had helped us write. We printed it out on blue paper and made it into a tri-fold so our friends could keep it handy. Though I had read this over many times, it was only as I reread it in preparation for Chaim's wedding that the parts of the wedding ceremony started to make sense.

Kabbalat Panim (Greeting)

Penina, the *kallah* (bride), will great her guests before the wedding ceremony begins. Although both men and women will be invited to join the *kallah* at this time, it is customary for only the women to hug, kiss, or shake hands with the bride.

Yehuda, the *chassan* (groom), will be sitting with his friends in another area or room called the *Chassan's Tish* where he will be involved with many of the legalities of the wedding.

Next the *ketubah* (marriage contract) will be filled out and signed by two witnesses. At this time Yehuda and Penina will make a *kinyan* (a token exchange) to solidify the agreement. In many cases, a handkerchief is used for the *kinyan*.

Bedecken (Veiling the Bride)

Many people consider this to be the most exciting part of the day. Yehuda will be led by his male friends and family in a singing and dancing procession toward Penina. Imagine how excited Penina and Yehuda will be. They will have not seen each other for seven days. One explanation for these days of separation is as simple as absence makes the heart grow fonder. As Yehuda approaches Penina, he will draw her veil over her face. One explanation for this custom is passed down from our matriarch Rivka who veiled herself in modesty the first time Yitzchak saw her face. Another possible explanation for veiling the bride goes back to Jacob who worked for seven years for Rachel's father, Laban, in order to be granted permission to marry her. Brides at that time wore thick veils and the grooms did not get to see them before the wedding. That's how Laban was able to trick Jacob into marrying Rachel's sister Leah. Thus Yehuda will make sure to see his bride, Penina, before the wedding ceremony.

Chupah (Wedding Canopy)

According to the *Talmud*, a marriage is to be completed under a *chupah* that symbolizes the new home that Yehuda and Penina plan to build together. Their family and friends will surround the *chupah* to show the world they will not build their home in isolation. The *chupah* is open on all four sides to show that their new home will always be open to others.

Yehuda will be wearing a *kittel* (white garment) as a symbol of purity. After a procession towards the *chupah* by members of the wedding party, Penina will be led there by her parents. Upon arriving under the *chupah*, Penina will proceed to walk around Yehuda seven times. According to Jewish tradition, the number seven symbolizes completion and fulfillment.

The wedding ceremony will begin with the *Keddushin* (sanctification). Two blessings will be recited. The first is a blessing over wine. The second praises *Hashem* (God) for the sanctity of marriage. Penina and Yehuda will share a cup of wine in order to mark the first of many shared experiences they will have in their life together.

Yehuda will then place the ring on Penina's forefinger, which is considered a direct pathway to her heart. After that, he will recite in Hebrew, "*Harei at medkudeshnet li. . .*" or "You are sanctified to me with this ring according to the laws of Moses and Israel." Once the *ketubah* is read aloud, Yehuda will hand it to Penina.

The next part of the ceremony is called the *Nissuin*, which seals the marriage. *Sheva Brachot* (seven blessings) will be recited over a second cup of wine. The wedding ceremony will conclude with Yehuda breaking a glass in remembrance of the destruction of the *Beis HaMikdash*, the original Temple in Jerusalem.

20

When to Arf Arf

An *aufruf* is the ceremony during which a bridegroom is called up to recite blessings over the *Torah*.

"Think Yehuda's going to have an *aufrif*?" Peter asked me a few weeks before the wedding.

"Why not?" I said. "You had one and you're not even Orthodox."

"Remember how we used to call it an arf-arf?"

I phoned Yehuda.

"You're going to have an *aufruf*, aren't you?" I asked him.

"Of course," he replied.

"I just wanted to be sure," I said, "Before I mention it to our rabbi. Doesn't it have to be on the Saturday before the wedding?"

"You got it, Mom. But . . . what's your rabbi got to do with it?"

"It's going to be up here, isn't it?"

"What gave you that idea?"

"Your *bar mitzvah* was in our synagogue so I just assumed—"

"Hold on. Have you forgotten I'm Orthodox and your synagogue is Conservative?"

Should I have told him how much it hurt to hear him say "your synagogue"? Attuned as I was to Yehuda's emotions, I was sure that bringing up that topic would probably start an argument. Remembering the stresses that kept piling up when dealing with my own parents while planning Peter's and my wedding, I decided to keep my mouth shut on this issue. During the months that preceded our wedding, there were many times I was ready to give up on a big celebration and elope instead. Not wanting to alienate Yehuda one month before his wedding, I said nothing.

"Would it be asking too much for you to bend the rules a bit?" I heard Peter ask.

"I can't," Yehuda said. He sounded impatient. "Even if I could, the synagogue at home is too far to walk to and you know I won't ride on *Shabbos*." I wondered if he could stay at someone's house near the synagogue. "And," he continued, "I'm not comfortable with men and women praying together."

"You make it sound like we're not good enough," Peter said.

There was a pause.

"Sorry," Yehuda said, "I didn't mean to hurt your feelings."

Silence.

"By the way," Yehuda told us, "I spoke to Rabbi Katz. You can stay at his house on Friday since I would not want you driving in on Saturday morning."

"Seems like you've got it all figured out," I said, wiping away my tears.

I felt defeated as I hung up the phone.

Resting my head on Peter's shoulder, I asked, "What's wrong with us? Why do we have to do everything his way?"

"Nothing's wrong with us," Peter said, caressing my shoulder. "But we've got no choice here. Yehuda's the one calling the shots because he's having an Orthodox wedding."

"But I feel so left out."

"Me too."

Moving away from Peter so I could see his face, I asked, "Really? You never seem to care about any of this. How come you never mentioned this before?"

"Why bother? It's already a done deal. We're Conservative. Yehuda is Orthodox. We have to go along with him if we want to stay connected."

21

Not Quite Beyond Compare

The day of my friend Sharon's daughter's wedding, exactly one week before Yehuda's, I couldn't decide what to wear. The hot pink pants ensemble I'd purchased months ago for the occasion no longer seemed appropriate. According to Orthodox customs, pants were only for men, so how could I ever consider wearing them to a Jewish wedding, even a Conservative one? Then I tried to convince myself that just because Orthodoxy was right for Yehuda did not mean I had to dress modestly when he was not around. Unsure of my own identity, my feet were stuck in two separate worlds—the Orthodox world to which Yehuda belonged and the world in which we had raised him. How I wished there were someone to help me figure out who I was, where I belonged. But there was no one. Not even Peter who—after thirty-plus years of marriage—knew me better than anyone. No matter how many times I tried explaining to him about my conflicted emotions, he didn't get it.

"You ready yet?" Peter called out from downstairs. "They'll be married before we get there."

An hour had gone by and I still hadn't decided what to wear.

"Be right down," I yelled, rushing into a strapless black gown and tossing a black lace shawl over my shoulders.

Once we were in the car, Peter asked, "Everything okay?"

"Sure," I said.

"Nothing you want to talk about?"

"Are you any more religious now than you were before Yehuda became interested in Orthodoxy?"

"I don't feel different. Why?"

"I'm . . . not sure where I belong anymore. All the rules and rituals of Orthodoxy are fascinating, but I'm not sure if they're for me."

"When Yehuda was allergic to chicken, you just made something else for him."

"So?"

"Yehuda's Orthodox. That doesn't mean we have to be."

Peter was right. But I was still confused.

As I held his hand during the wedding ceremony, Peter whispered, "Don't try this next week."

"We won't even be sitting together," I whispered back.

As soon as the ceremony was over, the bride and groom kissed passionately.

Amid cries of *Mazel Tov* from those around me, I turned toward my husband and mouthed the words, "I can't believe they did that."

Looking puzzled, he asked, "What'd you expect them to do, shake hands?"

Following him into the banquet hall, I said, "Yehuda and Penina haven't even held hands yet."

"Their problem, not ours."

"I don't know why I'm turning into such a prude."

Whistling at my bare shoulders, Peter said, "In that outfit, you sure don't look like one."

Slipping off my shoes on the way home, I said, "That was a great party. Even though the food was not kosher."

"How do you know that?"

"Aren't you the one who ordered steak with extra butter sauce?"

"Forgot about that."

"Hard to believe the bride had the nerve to wear pure white after they've been living together for months."

Peter didn't respond.

"Do you think it's the pre-wedding jitters?"

"Sounds like you've got a lot of things to think through."

Falling asleep was difficult that night. So I grabbed a pad of paper and a pen from my night stand, turned on the light in the hall and wrote down the following list of the things that bothered me about my friend's daughter's wedding:

1. Bride and groom had lived together for years
2. Bride wore a strapless gown
3. Bride and groom held hands during entire ceremony
4. Men and women sat together for the ceremony and the reception
5. Men and women danced together
6. Rock music, female singer
7. No black hats in sight
8. Hardly any of the men wore *yarmulkes*
9. Non-kosher food

Under ordinary circumstances, none of those things would have bothered me. But with Yehuda's wedding the following week, I was still sorting through my feelings, trying to figure out which world I fit into. I felt myself changing. I did not like the way my identity was evolving. It wasn't like trying on different pairs of shoes. The way I looked at the world was different than the way it had been before Yehuda's religious transformation. I had developed a worldview that reflected not who I used to be, but who I was now. Things I probably wouldn't have noticed before Yehuda's religious transformation—a bride dressed in white after having co-habited with the groom for nine years—now caught my attention. Had I become a prude? My father had accused me of that during my teenage years whenever I covered my ears at the sound of someone cursing or telling a dirty joke. Dirty jokes no longer troubled me. Swear words were part of my vocabulary. Nonetheless, I was troubled by not knowing who I had become. Did being the mother of two Orthodox sons mean I had to see the world from their perspective? No way! I wasn't even sure how they viewed the world. We are not the same and they are not the same. Each of my sons is a different person. They are themselves. I am me. I am proud that each has the self-confidence and character to follow his own path away from Peter's and mine.

I liked myself a lot better when I wasn't so critical of other people's choices. What gave me the right to judge other people so harshly? Given a choice, I'd rather be more accepting and less critical. Maybe that's one reason I've become more accommodating and accepting of our sons' needs as Orthodox men. I did not like the me I had become. But who exactly was that me? Would I ever rid myself of the critical eye I had acquired and through which I viewed the rest of the world? I was troubled by these questions.

And then there was Peter, who—except for watching his language and wearing a *yarmulke* when around our sons—was pretty much the same person he'd always been. I loved him for that. When I asked if he believed in God, his answer didn't surprise me, "There must be a Supreme Being who created the world because man could not do it all himself."

But when it came to the Orthodox, Peter told me, "They have too many rules. Taking time out for their families on *Shabbos* is wonderful. Some even have their kids living in their neighborhood. That's a good thing. They're a wonderful, caring community. They take care of each other. *Davening* three times a day! Who has time for that? The intellectual part is okay. I would not mind taking time out two or three days a week, one hour each night studying *Talmud*. What I don't like are so many rules. They have rules for everything. Can't clear the table until after *Shabbos*. But sitting at the table with dirty dishes staring you in the face is not a good thing."

The day after her daughter was married, I called Sharon to say we enjoyed the wedding.

"The problems I had with the other side." she told me. "They're so infuriating!"

"I know," I said, not in the mood for a rehash of her complaints.

"By the way, I was just looking at the info you sent out with Yehuda's wedding invitation. Where'd you learn all that?"

"Some from Yehuda and Penina. But we talk to Penina's parents almost every night."

"Hard to believe with you and Peter not Orthodox."

"We get along great!"

"Who planned the wedding, you or them?"

"Pretty much they did. But always asked for our input."

"What'd you tell them?"

"They raised such a wonderful daughter that we trust them to make the right choices."

I would have loved to tell Sharon about my conflicted emotions about her daughter's wedding, but did not want her to feel that I looked down on her because my children are religious and hers are not. My identity was the real issue, not knowing where I belonged. I was down on myself, but would not be able to claim my identity until I began that costume change in the restrooms of airplanes to and from Israel. That was how I found my way through the confusion as to who I was. Sometimes I was Yehuda and Chaim's mother, which required certain behaviors and a veneer of Orthodoxy. Inside I was the same down-to-earth woman as before. It was then that I started to realize I could be myself even while wearing something I felt was overly modest.

At Yehuda's wedding, it came to me that although everyone was all covered up on the outside, on the inside they had the same feelings and concerns and were really no different than I was.

My identity issues are pretty much resolved, but sometimes, especially during visits with my sons and their families, I still wonder what it would be like to live in the Orthodox world on a regular basis. Do I have what it takes to dress modestly all the time, to sleep in a separate bed from my husband, to keep *Shabbos,* to obey all 613 commandments, or at least the ones that apply to women? After pondering these issues for a second or two, I tell myself that I could do all those things but am happy to have a choice. I do not need to prove myself. I'm delighted with my life just as it is.

22

A Crash Course in Cramming

Packing for Yehuda's wedding was no problem for Peter; all he needed was a suit and a few dress shirts. For me, there was the powder blue silk suit and matching hat trimmed with pastel ribbon for the *aufruf* on Saturday, the regal blue gown and hat for the wedding on Sunday, and the suits for the *sheva brachot*, festive meals, during the week following the wedding. Several dressy suits hung in my closet. I picked the ones with skirts long enough to cover my knees while seated: the navy blue with white lapels, the black with the flowing skirt, and the brown with the short jacket and pencil skirt. And my stylish black straw hat.

Driving on *Shabbos* wasn't a problem for us, but it was for Yehuda. So instead of driving to Forest Pines on Saturday, we spent Friday night with Yehuda and Chaim at Rabbi Katz's. That way we could walk to the synagogue on Saturday morning for Yehuda's *aufruf*. After *Shabbos* we would drive to a hotel in Brooklyn to rest up for the wedding on Sunday. Chaim would take care of accommodations for after *Shabbos* for Yehuda and himself.

Friday evening is a blur. What I do recall is Saturday morning in Rabbi Katz's synagogue. Seated next to his wife Shuba in the women's section of the synagogue, the front of the sanctuary was barely visible. Hardly able to see Yehuda's handsome face or hear his slightly off-key voice as he chanted the blessings, I could not help but feel alone. The smiles of women seated around me had no effect on my feeling of isolation. I felt out-of-place and underdressed, the only one with a hat when everyone else was wearing a *sheitel*.

After the *aufruf,* I walked out of the synagogue and met up with Chaim and Peter.

Yehuda was surrounded by well-wishers.

A Tie, in Case

According to Orthodox tradition, the groom asks someone to be his *shomer*, to keep him company for the 24 hours preceding the wedding and take care of any last-minute issues that might come up. Yehuda chose Chaim. I was grateful that their religious beliefs had brought them closer. Chaim had just graduated from the University of Pennsylvania and was leaving for Israel soon after the wedding.

When the phone rang in our hotel room early Sunday, the day of the wedding, it surprised me to hear Chaim's voice on the end of the line.

"Everything okay?" I asked. "You sound tired."

"Yehuda's driving me nuts," said Chaim. "On the way to Brooklyn last night, he made me stop at Macy's to buy a tie and two dress shirts."

"An Orthodox custom?"

"No! He wants to have extras, just in case."

"Must be nervous."

"Fell asleep in his clothes."

The clock on the night table in our hotel room said eight o'clock.

"Is he awake yet?" I asked.

"Got me up at five."

"Want to meet for breakfast?"

"He's fasting."

"How come?"

"Today is like Yom Kippur for the bride and groom so they can get married with a clean slate."

"The wedding's not till tonight."

"Don't worry, Mom. He'll be okay."

There was shouting in the background.

"Gotta go," Chaim said and hung up.

Before we left for the catering hall, Peter adjusted his paisley tie in the full-length mirror. Standing beside him, I was delighted by my own reflection. The royal blue silk gown made me look marvelous.

"You look beautiful," Peter said, "But too covered up for my taste."

I felt my cheeks flush.

Soon after their wedding date was set, Yehuda and Penina had sent us a book, *Made in Heaven, A Jewish Wedding Guide*, by Rabbi Aryeh Kaplan. Peter skimmed it. I read it. However, instead of the "Cliff's Note Guide to Orthodox Weddings" I had hoped for, it was way too technical. Out of frustration, I took notes.

With Peter waiting to leave for the wedding, I took a tiny red notebook out of my handbag and leafed through the dog-eared pages of notes, nervously trying to memorize it all.

"Can't you just go with the flow?" Peter asked, sounding impatient.

"You know I like to be prepared."

"It's time to go."

I put the notebook back in my purse.

The outside of the Concordia—somewhere in Brooklyn—was unimpressive, but inside the perspective changed. The hallway, carpeted in various shades of beige, complemented the lushly patterned gold and brown wallpaper. Where was everyone? Finally someone showed up to take me to the bride's room.

"Mind if I leave you here?" I asked Peter.

Yehuda's around somewhere," he said confidently. We embraced. Brushing off the collar of his white shirt, he added, "Don't get any lipstick on my collar."

"I'm not wearing any. Penina's mom hired a professional to do our makeup."

Standing in the doorway of the bride's room, Penina was exquisite! Her ash brown hair curled gently at her shoulders. How could she think of hiding it under a *sheitel* after today, even if Orthodox modesty required her to do so? And her gown! Crafted of white organza, the jewel-necked bodice, fitted sleeves and high waist were ornamented by white-on-white embroidered flowers accented in silver; the inverted pleats of the skirt widened as they reached the floor releasing yards of flowing fabric.

I stood mesmerized until she hugged me tightly saying, "Mom, I'm so happy to see you. You look fantastic."

Forty-five minutes later, after the cosmetician finished applying my makeup—moisturizer, foundation, blusher, eyeliner on both upper and lower lids, and two shades of eye shadow, followed by a coating of mascara—I hardly recognized myself.

Malka appeared in a black and gold lame gown. I had never seen her looking so elegant. We embraced warmly and wished each other *Mazel Tov.*

After escorting Penina into the reception room, we helped her settle on a white high-backed wicker chair trimmed with miniature white roses. Her poise amazed me. Instead of being flustered when people arrived early, she welcomed them warmly.

Standing on one side of Penina, with Malka on the other, I felt awkward greeting so many people I did not know. Out of the 450 invited guests, at least 300 of them were Penina's family or friends. Finally, my college roommate appeared, followed by a few other familiar faces.

"Is that really you inside that gown and hat?" one of them asked me. I nodded. "If I didn't know better, I'd think you were Orthodox."

My identity crisis was far from over. Her comment only added to my confusion.

Even so, I whispered in her ear, "I guess I've learned how to dress the part."

The reception was open to both women and men. I worried that some of our guests would forget that it was inappropriate for the men to hug, kiss or shake hands with Penina. But everyone seemed to remember.

Before long, there was the sound of men's voices singing in Hebrew. They were coming closer. There was Yehuda being led by his best friends. He looked a little pale—probably from fasting all day—but oh so happy!

As he got closer, Penina's expression turned serious.

For a long moment, Yehuda stood directly in front of his bride, looking deeply into her eyes. Then, without a sideward glance, he reached toward her mother who handed him the *dek tichel*, a special thick white cloth meant to provide the bride with complete privacy. Using long hatpins, Yehuda gingerly attached it to the top of Penina's veiled headpiece. Penina's head bowed as if weighed down, her posture was no longer relaxed. I wondered if she was praying.

After Yehuda backed away, Shloime, Penina's grandfathers, and several other male relatives each said a blessing over Penina's bowed head. Next on line was Peter. Too bad I couldn't hear what he was saying. A few minutes later, the men started singing again and parading Yehuda out of the room.

As the reception was winding down, Peter came to get me.

"It's time to marry off our son," he said, somberly.

"Where is he?" I asked.

Leading me up a flight of stairs, he said, "Rabbi Katz wanted to talk to him."

A door opened. Yehuda emerged wearing a thin white cloth robe over his dark suit, and carrying a black raincoat.

"Expecting rain?" I asked.

"This is a *kittel*," he said, holding the lapels of his robe. "The same one I started wearing on Yom Kippur as a sign of purity."

"What's with the raincoat?"

The look on his face told me he did not know the answer. All he said was that there was a tradition in some families to wear a black raincoat over the *kittel*.

Helping our son into the raincoat, Peter asked, "What's on your forehead? Forgot to wash your face?"

Smiling weakly, Yehuda explained, "As Jews, no matter how happy we are, we can't forget the tragedies that affected us in the past." He said that Rabbi Katz had let a candle burn for a few minutes and then had blown it out in order to have ashes to place on Yehuda's forehead as a reminder of the Temple that was destroyed over 3,000 years ago.

The wedding day is the start of a new beginning for the bridal couple. Tradition holds that the gates of heaven are more open to their prayers on this special day so it is not uncommon for the bride and groom to pray for a good married life, good health for those who are ill, and help for those who need it.

As Peter and I accompanied Yehuda down the aisle toward the *chupah*, we had to strain to hold him up. His lips moved but no sound came out. I assumed he was praying, but in no way did that stop me from worrying he would pass out during the ceremony. Once we reached the *chupah*, he did perk up a bit.

Looking out at the throng of guests, men on one side, women on the other, I scanned the crowd hoping to find anyone I knew. But I was so nervous in front of all those people that all I saw was a blur. Too bad there had been no rehearsal or I might have been able to prime myself for being on display. In the back of my mind, I kept hoping to not do anything that might embarrass Yehuda or Penina.

Malka took her daughter's arm and started walking her around Yehuda, who seemed in prayer. Despite my note taking, I had no idea whether I was supposed to take part in this procession or not. So I took a chance and gathered up the train of Penina's gown—as it turned out, that was exactly what I was supposed to do—and followed her and her mother to the accompaniment of someone chanting in Hebrew.

Later Yehuda placed a plain gold band—symbolizing eternity—on Penina's right index finger. Once the ceremony was completed, she was free to move it to the ring finger on her left hand. After several blessings from the rabbi, Penina and Yehuda took sips of wine. The rabbi then unrolled the marriage contract and read it aloud. Next, the seven blessings were recited.

The ceremony ended with Yehuda stomping on a glass—that was wrapped in a napkin—in memory of the loss of the first Temple in Jerusalem.

I let out a deep breath.

Someone escorted Penina and Yehuda to a room where they could have a few minutes of privacy and break their fast.

Pretty soon, the newlyweds appeared in the doorway. Faces beaming. Eyes glistening. Shouts of *Mazel Tov* seemed to come from every corner of the ballroom. Though Penina had taken off the heavy veil at the conclusion of the wedding ceremony, the sequined tiara she had worn underneath it continued to grace her head. While Yehuda, still sporting the new black hat he bought for the occasion, gradually disappeared into the men's side of the *mechitza*, Penina tried to make her way to the women's side.

No sooner had she taken a few steps into the room when some of her friends rushed toward her holding pastel-colored plastic arches in their outstretched arms. There was no symbolism attached to the arches except that it was customary to treat the bride as a queen. To the accompaniment of loud cheers, Penina lowered her head, passing under each arch. Before she could get to her seat, the band started playing something lively.

As soon as her mother and sister joined her in the center of the room, a circle formed around them. Within moments, it seemed as if all 175 of us women wanted a chance to dance with the bride. I hadn't realized there were so many circle dances. Once Penina reached for my hand, I stopped feeling self-conscious and moved in time with the music.

Sometime later, I was surprised to have Peter turn up and offer to bring me to the men's side.

"It's against the rules," I protested.

"Penina's already there. Doesn't that make it okay?"

I gave in.

Sure enough, when we got to the men's side, Penina was seated a few feet away from Yehuda watching one of his friends dance, a full bottle of vodka on his head. As I stood there gaping, the dancer lowered his head, caught the glass bottle in his hands, tore off the seal, opened it and drank heartily.

Next, a distinguished-looking man dashed into the center of the circle that had formed around Yehuda. Without hesitation, this man hopped on a unicycle and began to juggle four rubber balls. Someone doing a wild dance while carrying another man on his shoulders was next.

Much too soon, the main course was served. So Peter escorted me back to the women's side.

Taking my seat next to Malka, I said, "You won't believe what's happening on the men's side."

"I'm not surprised," she said.

"You mean it's common for guys to dance with bottles on their heads?"

"Things tend to get a bit crazy at weddings."

"But it's so calm on the women's side."

"Penina warned her friends not to do any 'funny stuff.' She doesn't want any injuries."

I looked at Malka, questioningly.

"The girls sometimes fill up balloons with confetti and the bride chases them with a hat pin. Or they make her a jump rope out of cloth napkins tied together."

"That doesn't sound dangerous."

"You'd be surprised."

There were bottles of dry white and full-bodied red wine on every table, but I don't remember having any. Wine sometimes goes to my head. I didn't want to miss out on any of the wedding.

After a few sips of water, I told Malka, "I thought women were never allowed on the men's side."

"It depends," Malka said. "As far as we women are concerned, watching a man dance is not the least bit erotic." Giving that some thought, I realized she wasn't talking about the Chippendales. "On the other hand," she continued, "A man watching a woman dance could be considered quite suggestive."

There was a lot more dancing after the main course.

Peter didn't come looking for me again until the guests started leaving at 11:30.

Before the newlyweds left for their hotel, Yehuda hugged me tightly.

Tears in his eyes, he said, "I love you Mom. Thanks for believing in me."

24

Knowing How to Say No

The week after the wedding, Chaim went to Israel to participate in a summer program that involved an *ulpan*, an intensive Hebrew immersion program, in the morning and working in a Jewish soup kitchen in the afternoon. I was totally impressed, not only because he wanted to improve his knowledge of Hebrew but because he was going to spend part of his time helping others. That was so Chaim.

While in high school, he had told me that Conservative Judaism was "pushing off assimilation for one more generation." His Jewish friends had no interest in dating Jewish girls. Their parents forced them to go to Hebrew school "out of obligation, not out of belief in the value of it." They dropped their kids off for services on Saturday morning but never sat through the services themselves. "Their kids had to suffer just as the parents had once suffered." Chaim went on to say that Judaism was important to him because Yehuda was becoming Orthodox, and because Peter and I were not like his friends' parents. We brought our sons to services and stayed there with them.

During high school, Chaim looked for a place to volunteer. A local agency set him up with an adult who had dropped out of high school and wanted to get his high-school-equivalency diploma. Chaim worked with this guy once a week for several years. By the time Chaim started college, the guy had earned his diploma. During college, Chaim made a point of spending a few hours every week visiting patients at a nearby hospital.

In the afterglow of Yehuda's wedding, Peter and I drove Chaim to the airport. When Yehuda and Chaim had started going to sleep-away camp, I had spent a few summers studying in France and Spain with the goal of improving my own linguistic ability. So Chaim spending the summer in Israel learning to speak Hebrew sounded right to me.

This was July 2001, months before the terrorist attack on the United States, but more than one year into the second Intifada in Israel. Though I was usually up on the news, during the past year I had paid less attention to the ongoing issues in Israel because Yehuda was back in the States. So it wasn't until Peter tuned in the news on our way home from the airport that I started to connect the terror of the suicide bombings in Israel with the reality that Chaim was on his way there. *How could I have agreed to let him go?* As we pulled into the rest area on the Thruway, Peter told me I looked pale. I opened my mouth, but no words came out.

"How could we let him go to that dangerous place?" I asked Peter, when I found my voice. "Why didn't we stop him?"

" You've known about it for months," Peter said.

"Wasn't paying attention. Must have let the wedding distract me from my better judgment."

"Couldn't have talked him out of going."

"At least I could have tried."

In January 2002, the Palestinians were exerting enormous pressure on Israel to release its hold on both Gaza and the West Bank. Ambushes and suicide bombings were commonplace. No matter. Peter and I packed our bags to visit Chaim. Determined to not let the Palestinians keep me away from our son, I was more worried about Chaim's welfare than my own. But the last days before we left, I started to feel anxious. The phone kept ringing with friends and family, including Penina's parents, wishing us a safe trip. On the way to the airport, we stopped to see Yehuda and Penina. They gave us money to donate to charities in Israel, saying it was a way to insure that we would have a safe trip.

On the plane, I met a woman who had survived the attempted hijacking of an Israeli passenger plane by the Palestine Liberation Organization in 1974.

"If it hadn't been standard procedure to lock the cockpit door on every Israeli passenger plane," she said, "who knows what would have happened?"

It was hard to keep myself from thinking about that during our long flight.

Chaim met us at the airport. He looked great. How I wished I could keep him safe!

After a troublesome attempt at sleep the night of our arrival, we took a walking tour of the southern wall of the ancient Temple. Our guide spoke no English, so Chaim acted as our translator. His command of Hebrew was amazing! But he seemed to thrive on arguing with the taxi drivers over their rates. This haggling grew so heated during one ride that the taxi started to swerve and I got nauseous.

I was struck by the way Israel had responded to the violence over the past year. Wherever we went, police or soldiers made their presence known. The economy was in terrible shape. The only visitors seemed to be people like Peter and me, who had specific reasons to be there. Three brand new hotels never opened due to a lack of tourists. A guest at our hotel heard an explosion while shopping in the tourist area of Jerusalem. The next day he found out that a Jewish man and the female suicide bomber had been killed in the blast.

When I wrote in my travel journal that I didn't feel uncomfortable or scared, I was only trying to reassure myself that we were all safe. What really bothered me was that Chaim showed no concern for the possible dangers of being in that country at that time.

The bleating of ambulances was not uncommon. The hotel manager told us that one ambulance was not usually cause for concern. But the sound of multiple ambulances meant, "You should call your family to ensure that everyone has been accounted for. You hang up immediately to keep the phone lines clear."

Most Israelis were labeled either "right" or "left" depending on their opinions of the Palestinian uprising, which had been going on for sixteen months. Those on the right wanted the Palestinians kicked out of the West Bank and Gaza. Those on the left sympathized with the Palestinian cause. This caused tremendous tension between friends and family members.

My cousin moved his family to Israel in the 1950s. His children gradually grew apart, both emotionally and geographically, due to their differing beliefs. One daughter was "far left." Living in a safe, seaside town in the northern part of Israel, she was willing to give up everything for peace.

"We live our lives normally, but the Palestinians have no normal life. Thirty-three years under occupation is horrendous!" she told me.

Her older sister wanted to live peacefully in Jerusalem with her Arab neighbors but was unsure whom to trust, afraid to open her door to strangers.

"I worry, shake and can't sleep whenever I hear about a suicide bombing," she said. "I want my freedom back! I can put up with anything as long as I have a hope and a dream. The dream of peace is breaking!"

Both sisters found it impossible to visit their brother, who was "far right" and lived in what was known to some people as "occupied land" in Gaza. Carrying a gun for protection, he insisted he would never surrender his home.

"The Palestinians are like a cancer in our bodies," he said. "We need to take out the bad cells to become well. What if Mexico suddenly insisted that the United States return California? That's how I feel about the occupied territories."

Little did he know that in 2005 Israel would turn over Gaza to the Palestinians, forcing him to move.

Chaim was enrolled at a *yeshiva* on the West Bank and wanted us to see it. After a suicide bombing early that morning, security was extra tight at the bus station in Jerusalem. We took an armored, bulletproof bus to the West Bank. Soldiers were scattered among the passengers. Several seemed barely old enough to shave, but their presence was reassuring. The bus took the shorter route that passed Arab villages. On days when there was shooting from those villages, it was forced to take a much longer route. But life went on as usual. The sun continued to shine brightly. Traffic sped by us. People chatted about the latest suicide bombing and then went on with their lives. A billboard in Hebrew, English and Arabic said, "Better to have pains of peace than agonies of war."

Heavy fog made it hard to see the few tiny roses in bloom outside the entrance to the main building of the *yeshiva*. Inside the door was a guard with an Uzi. The *beis midrash*, the main sanctuary that was also used as a study hall, was a large rectangular room with long tables facing a podium behind which the *rosh*, the chief rabbi, or other rabbis stood to deliver their *shiurim*, lectures. Chaim introduced us to a few of his rabbis who spoke English and went on to tell us how impressed they were with our son, "especially when he's not falling asleep."

Lunch was in the cafeteria. A few other women were there. Most of the guys carried plates heaped with fried fish balls, schnitzel, corn kernels and mashed potatoes, taboule, and tossed salad. Some had bowls of soup that sloshed as they walked to their seats. One had a pyramid of corn kernels covering his plate, reminding me of a collegiate football player filling up on carbs before a big game.

I wanted more time with Chaim, but our week together was almost over. He wanted to get back to his learning. We had a plane to catch. I was pretty sure any effort to push Chaim to come back to the United States would be met with a firm refusal. No matter, I gave it a try.

"I know you want to prove you can take care of yourself," I said. "But the world isn't the same place it was before you left. So please come back."

"Israelis know how to protect their public buildings," said Chaim. "Americans are just learning how. I'm safer here than you are in the States."

"We love you so much. We don't want anything to happen to you!"

"I'm a big boy now! I can take care of myself!"

He refused to discuss how long he planned to stay. He wanted time to study at the *yeshiva*, but would keep in touch. When he was ready, he would come back to the States to work on a graduate degree.

Being a parent was teaching us a difficult truth. In the end we had no control over the paths our sons chose.

Before tearfully leaving the *yeshiva*, I watched Peter write out a few rules for Chaim to follow:

1. Come home if you need to.
2. Don't go into the tourist areas of Jerusalem.
3. Stay within the fenced-in community of the *yeshiva* as much as possible.
4. Call us whenever there's a terrorist situation to tell us you're safe.
5. Stay safe.

Chaim signed the list, for all the good it did. Maybe it made Peter feel better but it didn't make me happy about leaving my son in such a dangerous part of the world.

In the bulletproof bus on our way back to Jerusalem, I watched a teenager hand the driver a brown paper bag before she walked to her seat. That made me nervous. Unidentified packages were not permitted on the bus! But the driver placed the bag on the windowsill next to his seat.

"Did you see that bag?" I asked Peter who was dozing.

Rubbing his eyes, he asked, "What bag? What's the problem?"

I nervously pointed out the bag and explained about the girl who had given it to the driver, but Peter told me that I worry too much. He said the girl was probably the driver's daughter and the bag probably contained the driver's dinner. Sure enough, a little later, the driver opened the bag and took out a sandwich.

The next day, on the way to the airport, we stopped at the Wailing Wall so I could place a note between the ancient stones, asking that Chaim be kept safe.

After we landed safely in the States, there was news of a bombing at Sbarro's in Jerusalem, Chaim's favorite place for pizza. My heart pounded. When we spoke to Chaim, he mentioned having walked past Sbarro's several minutes before the blast, so he was "a bit shaken up." I was ready to get on the next plane back to Israel. But Peter insisted we not emasculate Chaim by demanding he come home immediately.

Chaim tried to placate me when he came home for Passover, by investigating a *yeshiva* in New York, but nothing about that place met his expectations. Though the situation in Israel was worsening daily, he was intent on returning. When I called Penina's parents and the Katzes for advice, they said that the area where Chaim's *yeshiva* was located was one of the safest places in all of Israel. After he left, there were times I woke up in the middle of the night petrified that something had happened to him He was on a battlefield! There was no way to know which area of Israel would be hit next. Imagine my relief a few months later when he moved back to the States, found an apartment in New York City and started looking for a job.

25

Walking the Line Without
an Instruction Book

Yehuda and Penina stayed with us for a few days during the month after their wedding. Having been told that Orthodox couples sleep in separate beds, I bought twin beds for Yehuda's room and offered to change the Star Wars wallpaper, but Yehuda said not to bother. His college texts and reference books filled the bookcases on one side of the room; religious texts overflowed the other; magic tricks were in a big box in the top of the closet; and CDs and cassettes were piled up on the shelves of his stereo.

After one night in his old room, they asked to move to the guest room for the rest of their stay. According to Yehuda, it was inappropriate for a married couple to sleep in the same room where religious books were stored. Peter and I offered to move the books, but Yehuda insisted on keeping them where they were.

Yehuda and Penina did not stop smiling at each other the entire time they were at our house. They were so cute together, calling each other pet names like sweetie pie, lovey, and darling, as if they were playing house.

Their new home was a rented two-bedroom apartment not far from Yehuda's *yeshiva*, so Penina commuted to the Jewish elementary school in Brooklyn. The kitchen in their apartment had two large sinks—one meat, one dairy—a side-by-side refrigerator, and a gas stove. A countertop separated the kitchen from the sparsely furnished main room that served as both living room and dining room. In preparation for *Shabbos*, the metal folding table that doubled as a workspace was covered with a white linen tablecloth friends had given them as a wedding gift. To prevent this special tablecloth from becoming stained by the traditional red *Shabbos* wine, they covered it with a clear plastic sheet. I didn't like the plastic effect, but it did serve a purpose. Besides, it wasn't up to me.

Two six-foot-high balsa wood bookcases, stained to look like cherry, lined the outside wall. I was proud of Yehuda and Penina for not investing in expensive furniture for their first apartment when they had no idea where they would end up.

In the balsa-wood bedroom, there was a high-riser that they insisted on separating into twin beds whenever we stayed. I asked why they persisted in this when they knew that Peter and I slept together at our home. They said it had to do with the laws of marital relations that require men and women to sleep in separate beds. I still didn't see why Peter and I had to follow the rules of Orthodox marital relations, but decided to not push it. I now see that if we had not started following those rules back then, we would have had a hard time following them when our yet-to-be born grandchildren were old enough to ask questions.

The small closet in the guest bedroom was filled with Penina's teaching clothes. Instead of asking for space for our stuff when we visited—usually every other month—Peter and I lived out of our suitcases, keeping them open on the floor between the beds. After Liba, our first grandchild, was born, we shared the guest room with her. In order to walk past her crib, we pushed our suitcases under the beds.

Penina planned elaborate meals for *Shabbos*. She made her own *challah*, chicken soup, roasted chicken, two marinated salads full of fresh vegetables, and yummy homemade non-dairy ice cream made with whatever berry she found at the local grocery. I borrowed many of her recipes. For Saturday lunch, there was more of the same in addition to the *cholent* that was kept heated on the gas stovetop with a foil-covered metal tray over the pilot light. By Saturday evening, something—usually chunks of *cholent*—invariably spilled on the top of the stove, seeping into the gas burners.

The dishes were rinsed with cold water—there was something about not using anything but cold water on *Shabbos*—and then piled on the counter. I always offered to wash the dishes with soap—and cold water—after dinner, but Yehuda and Penina insisted that could wait until the next morning. They had their own rules. I tried to keep from pushing them to do things my way.

However, one Saturday night after *Shabbos* was over and all the dishes were washed in hot water and put away, Yehuda and Penina decided to go for a walk. While they were gone, I decided to clean the top of the stove, thinking I was doing something nice for Penina.

Using an abrasive sponge and detergent, I spent an hour scrubbing and then showed off to Peter who told me, "Penina will be so happy to see what you've done."

But later that evening when Penina put up a pot of water for tea, instead of thanking me, she ignored me, whispered to Yehuda, walked into her bedroom, and closed the door.

"Mom, I can't believe you cleaned the stove," Yehuda said, sounding disappointed.

"Just trying to help," I said, proudly.

"You thought you were. But you weren't!"

"All I did was scrub until my fingers started getting numb. Is that a crime?"

"Penina has her own way of doing things after *Shabbos*. Cleaning the stove without asking is like having someone dump your dinner in the trash without asking if you're finished."

I'd been trying so hard to not be a meddling mother-in-law but it had happened anyway.

"I . . . did not mean to interfere."

Much later, Penina emerged from her bedroom.

Looking doleful, she said, "Mom, I know you were only trying to help, but . . ."

"I'm so sorry," I said, wiping my eyes. "This is your home. I should have asked you before I did anything."

Tears in our eyes, we hugged.

26

A Skirt and Skis

The only reason I learned to ski was because Peter loved it. Yehuda also loved it, so Penina wanted to learn. I couldn't picture her skiing. Not that she was awkward or clumsy, but most Orthodox woman didn't wear pants. How could she ski in a skirt?

No matter. When Yehuda asked to spend the weekend with us and then went on to ask if I would babysit on Sunday so that Penina could take a ski lesson, of course I said yes. Having them visit was always wonderful. Having my two month-old granddaughter to myself for a few hours was a bonus.

With the early start of *Shabbos* during the winter months, there was little time on Friday afternoon to make plans for Sunday. So we waited until *Shabbos* was over on Saturday night. That was when I found out that it's okay for a religious woman to wear pants as long as she wears a skirt on top. Penina wore a *sheitel* and a tailored grey skirt suit for *Shabbos*. Afterwards, she replaced her *sheitel* with a *snood*, and changed into a comfortable knit skirt. I was caught off-guard when she asked to try on my ski pants. She really looked silly with a skirt on top of my black ski pants. But I kept my mouth shut. If that was what she had to do to conform to religious standards, it wasn't my place to comment. We all make concessions when it comes to keeping warm.

The next morning at Gore Mountain, Peter and Yehuda toted the ski equipment to the lodge while Penina and I arranged for her lesson. Until she brought it up, I didn't realize that she wanted a female instructor—not because there was anything wrong with a male in-structor but just in case the instructor needed to touch her to help her get into the right position.

After Penina left with her female instructor and Yehuda and Peter went off to ski, I pushed the stroller with my sleeping granddaugh-ter toward the window facing the beginner ski slope and settled in to watch Penina learn to ski. Every so often, I snapped a picture of her leaning from one leg to the other, and then forward and back. She seemed to be enjoying herself, gaining confidence with every stride. Pretty soon she was gliding instead of just pushing the skis in the snow. Every so often, she waved at me, a big smile under the ski helmet. The lesson was scheduled to last an hour, but the instructor gave her an extra fifteen minutes. As I watched, Penina started moving down the gentle beginner slope, gaining speed as she went past the lodge. A few minutes later, she entered the lodge, covered with snow.

"That was great," she told me. "Too bad I did not learn how to stop."

Later on Peter babysat while Penina and I took the gondola to the top of the mountain to watch Yehuda ski. That way she was able to see another side of her religious husband.

27

Perfection is Flawless

Our first grandchild was born in the fall of 2002. I couldn't wait to meet her. I knew I might be a grandmother someday but never gave any weight to the wonders of my own child having a child. On the way to the hospital, we stopped for a bouquet of flowers and a balloon that said, "It's a Girl."

Penina looked exhausted but happy. Hospital food was okay, but she wanted fresh fruit. So while Peter took Yehuda back to his apartment to shower, Malka and I went for fruit. Though fresh fruit is kosher, it has to be cut with a kosher knife. Hoping to present Penina with a platter and not just a bag of fruit, Malka and I went in search of a kosher store that sold fruit. The shopkeeper said if we could wait an hour, he'd prepare a platter for us. But we didn't have an hour. So we bought a cantaloupe, a small watermelon, two apples, two peaches, a pear and an orange, and asked him to let us cut it ourselves.

"Fine by me," came the reply.

"Do you have a platter we can use?"

All he had were for the orders he had yet to fill.

So we dashed across the street for a plastic platter, and then back to the fruit store where the shopkeeper lent us a paring knife. We were both so excited about our new granddaughter that we giggled incessantly throughout the entire escapade.

There is a custom in Penina's family and ours to not buy anything for a baby until after it is born. So before Malka and I went back to the hospital, we bought baby clothes.

It is hard to describe the ecstasy I felt while holding my granddaughter for the first time. There she was, all curled up, soft, and snuggly.

The naming of baby girls takes place in the synagogue during the reading of the *Torah*. Though Yehuda was only seven when Nana, my grandmother, died, I was delighted that he had wonderful memories of her and decided to name his daughter after her.

Liba's naming took place at one of the many synagogues in Penina's parents' neighborhood. As usual, I sat in the women's section that, in this case, was upstairs. There was a tiny opening in the center of the floor directly over the reader's table in the sanctuary. Although unable to see their faces, I could see the top of Yehuda's head and Peter's. And I was able to hear Yehuda chant his *aliyah* before and after the reading of the *Torah*. I later found out that Peter lifted the *Torah* just as high and wide as Yehuda had requested. After services, we adjourned to the social hall for the reception.

Chaim was now living in Washington Heights and still looking for a job. His field of expertise was centered on the human genome. He had no way of knowing that he would soon be hired to do research by the American Museum of Natural History, would graduate from the doctoral program in biology at New York University, and be married within a few years.

After almost two years in New Jersey, Yehuda and Penina said they were ready to buy a house there. That's why they caught us by surprise when they asked our permission to move to Israel. Yehuda said his allergies were bothering him so much that the doctor suggested moving to a warm, dry climate.

Letting them go might have been easier if it were just the two of them, but Liba was almost six months old. We didn't want them taking her so far away from us. On the other hand, what are parents supposed to do when their adult children want to go off on their own? Isn't this a continuation of the separation that begins at birth?

"It's only temporary," Yehuda assured us. "Not as if we're moving away forever."

"Sure feels that way," I said, sadly.

"Be back in the States in a year or two."

That was over seven years ago. Peter is still pestering Yehuda for a commitment, but I gave up on that a few years ago, realizing it was not doing any good. If and when they move back to the States, it will be because the time is right for them, not for us. The same holds true for if and when Yehuda decides to get a "real job."

Liba was born in October; Eva was born the following November, in Israel. So, a few days later, I flew to Israel to help out. I loved having Liba with me every morning starting promptly at 7:00 a.m. She repeated everything, even nonsense words I made up.

Trying to give Yehuda and Penina some time to themselves, I would go for a walk or retreat to my room—actually a winterized porch heated by the standing electric heater that I found at the local hardware store. Thank goodness it was on display in the store, because I had no idea how to say heater in Hebrew.

Peter arrived one week later, in time for Eva's naming. Unlike the catered meal at the synagogue in honor of Liba, the reception in honor of Eva was held in Yehuda and Penina's apartment. Most of the neighbors brought homemade treats. The dining room was set up for the men, with all sorts of cakes, pies and cookies. The women gathered in the kitchen to chat. Unfortunately, very few spoke English, so I felt left out of most of the conversation.

Blimi was born fourteen months later in January 2005. This time Malka and Shloime went to help. Peter and I arrived one week later. Penina's parents stayed in the apartment. Yehuda found a place for us a few blocks away. Malka and I bought fancy partyware at the paper goods store. Penina's friends took care of the cakes, candies, and *cholent*. The men celebrated in Yehuda and Penina's apartment. The women gathered in an apartment upstairs that belonged to Penina's friend. Most of the women spoke only Yiddish. Malka was able to talk with them, but there was no time to translate each conversation into

English. So I sat and smiled, feeling even more out of place than I had at the party in honor of Eva's birth.

I have gradually come to realize that, no matter what I try, deep inside I'll always be an outsider to the Orthodox community. It's not mine. I am just a visitor. I don't belong. It is not as if the Orthodox community went out of its way to snub me. Absolutely no one did anything of the sort. If I really wanted to try to fit in, I could start by wearing a *sheitel*. But dressing the part would not be enough for me. It would take years of study before I'd feel prepared to strictly observe all of the Orthodox rules and rituals in the appropriate manner.

Not knowing much Hebrew can be frustrating. I once considered participating in an *ulpan* but decided my time in Israel was better spent with my family. One afternoon, my husband and I were babysitting for our grandchildren when two children came to the door; they must have been four and six. One of them was holding a clear plastic cup. After the older one said something in Hebrew, the younger one held out the cup. *What did they want?* They were nicely dressed, but we assumed they were beggars. In that neighborhood it wasn't unheard of for people to ask for money. After my husband put a few *shekels* in the cup, both children looked surprised. *Had they expected more money?* Peter closed the door.

A few minutes later, there was a knock at the door. The children had returned with their older sister who spoke English.

"My mother said to thank you for the coins," she said. "But all she really wanted was a cup of flour."

It's not uncommon for Israeli mothers to give their four-year-olds a shopping list and money before sending them across the street to the convenience store. I was in the store once when this happened and was amazed at how well the child did on her own. She handed the clerk the list. The clerk assembled the items. The child paid and waited for the change.

A few days later, I volunteered to do a bit of shopping for Penina. Nothing much more than a few containers of yogurt and some butter were the items she needed. Even so, she wrote out a list for me.

My problem came when the clerk in the store asked me a question I didn't understand. I thought he wanted to know how many yogurts I needed, but later realized he was probably asking what flavor I needed. Arriving back at the apartment, I was embarrassed to learn that I had purchased the right number of yogurts, but the wrong flavor.

For now I've decided to hold off on any more attempts at learning Hebrew. I keep hoping Yehuda and Penina will return to the States.

"When are you going to stop this nonsense and come home?" Peter asked Yehuda during one of our visits.

Looking as if he were injured by the question, Yehuda said, "The study of *Torah* is not nonsense."

"When are you going to bring your family back to the United States and get a real job?"

"There you go again Dad! Studying *Torah* is 'a real job!'"

"I give up. When are you coming home?"

"Probably three more years at this *yeshiva* and two more somewhere else."

"So you'll be coming home in five years? Do I have that straight?"

"Maybe. It's not easy to say how much more time I'll need. Sorry, but that's how it is."

When I heard that, I started to wonder how we would survive five more years of trips to Israel. All that travel was becoming way too draining. The last time, our flight back home was delayed for ten hours.

28

Nowhere Near the Freezer

When Chaim started looking for a wife, I hoped he would not rush into a relationship with the first girl he met. After consulting several *shadchens*, none of the girls he met was the right one. He told me about a girl in his neighborhood. Although he had a lot in common with her, he would never date her, because her parents were divorced.

"Worried it will rub off?" I asked him.

He said it wasn't worth taking the chance.

Chaim joined an Orthodox synagogue and signed up for a singles' lunch group. It was there that he met Shulamit in October 2005.

"I met a girl," he told us

"That's nice," we said.

"We went out on Saturday."

"That's nice."

"And the Saturday before that."

"That's nice."

"And last Tuesday too."

"Are you trying to tell us something?"

"Maybe."

Instead of just sitting and talking to each other for hours in a hotel lobby—as Yehuda and Penina had done—Chaim took Shulamit to the video arcade in Times Square. Another night he took her to a showing of *The Rocky Horror Picture Show* at midnight at a theater in Manhattan.

Yehuda would probably not have approved of Chaim's dating rituals, but there was no reason to share them with him. Though it may seem that Chaim was making up his own rules, I doubt that this was so. Yehuda believes in adhering to all the rules to the nth degree. Chaim believes that some are open to interpretation. Yehuda believes in closing out a lot of the outside world, spending his time studying the *Torah*. Chaim splits his time between *Torah* study and working in a computer laboratory. Chaim's brand of Orthodoxy is much easier for me to deal with. Yehuda's took a lot more time for me to get used to. And I may not be there yet.

When Chaim was ready for us to meet Shulamit, we had dinner together at a kosher restaurant in his neighborhood. This was stripped of all the formality that Yehuda had put us through when we first met Penina in the lobby of the Holiday Inn in Monsey. Penina's parents came with her to meet us. But Shulamit met us with her parents nowhere in sight. Peter and I had to find our way to the restaurant by ourselves so that Chaim could pick up Shulamit. He had told me that red was her favorite color and that she liked to wear scarves. So I bought her a black and red plaid one with matching red earmuffs.

Shulamit's jet-black hair fell to her shoulders in soft curls that set off her porcelain complexion. In her off-white sweater set and a long black skirt, she looked covered-up, yet chic. Although I had prepared myself to like her no matter what, she was just as charming as Chaim had described.

"How did you know I love red?" Shulamit asked, her eyes grinning at Chaim as she gingerly removed the scarf from the box and wrapped it around her neck. "Thank you so much, Mrs. Rosenfeld. I really love it."

"I'm glad you like it," I said. "But would it be okay if you called me BJ?"

She said that was fine with her.

I remembered how thrilled I was when Penina asked if she could call me "Mom" that evening when Yehuda called to tell us that Penina had agreed to marry him. From the way Shulamit and Chaim looked at each other, it was clear to me that marriage was in the offing.

I was so happy that, turning toward Shulamit, the following words came out of my mouth, "And maybe sometime in the future you'll be able to call me 'Mom.'"

Nobody spoke.

Chaim groaned.

Shulamit smiled, weakly.

Peter kicked my leg.

I felt awkward.

"Sorry," I said. "I guess I misspoke."

With that, the waiter brought our menus. Once our orders were placed, Peter started to tell one of the truly corny jokes he's been telling ever since our boys were young. Way before Peter got to the punch line, Chaim put out his hand to stop him. *Had Chaim heard that one too many times? Or maybe he did not want Peter to embarrass himself in front of Shulamit by telling such a stupid joke.* I was wrong on both counts.

Stopping in mid-sentence, Peter frowned and then asked, "Something the matter?"

"I tried to tell that one last week," Chaim said, winking at Shulamit, "But Shulamit's already heard it too many times from her dad."

"As far as my dad's concerned, the cornier the better," Shulamit added.

"Join the club," I said, gesturing at Peter and Chaim.

Chaim had told us that Shulamit's religious background was similar to his, up to a point. He said that her parents are unpretentious, like Peter and me. They raised their daughter to be a good Conservative Jew and they keep a kosher home. Bacon—which used to be one of Chaim's favorite foods whenever we went out for breakfast—was something Shulamit had never tasted. She had never eaten any meat that was not kosher. Chaim went on to explain that contrary to where we live with no kosher restaurants, where there are plenty within a short driving distance of the Long Island community where Shulamit grew up.

When I asked Shulamit about becoming Orthodox, she said she finally gave up saying "No" to the rabbi at her college when he called to invite her to join his family for dinner on Friday night.

"That's all it took?" Peter asked.

"Not really," she said, "I was not a rebellious teenager. But by the time I got to high school, I was an atheist."

This was not what I expected to hear.

"How'd that happen?" I asked.

Looking thoughtful, she said, "I don't know. It just did."

"Were your parents okay with this?"

"They only went to services at synagogue on *Rosh Hashanah* and Yom Kippur, so my being an atheist was not a big deal for them."

Shulamit went on to say that even though she had stopped believing in God, she never took off the Jewish Star of David that she wore around her neck. As she said this, she tugged gently on the silver chain around her neck to show us a small silver six-sided star. She recalled having fingered it while giving an oral presentation on atheism in one of her high school history classes.

"When I pledged a sorority at college, they made me bow down in front of one of the sorority sisters. That was so weird! My mother had taught me never to bow down when I went to church with my friends, so why did I have to bow down now? And then they told me about the patron saint of the sorority and how she was going to protect me if I followed all the rules. A patron saint? I may have been an atheist, but that was not for me."

Shulamit told us that she got into singing when she was in sixth grade and it became her life during middle school and high school. While at the University of Maryland, she was privileged to perform at the Kennedy Center in Washington D.C. and Lincoln Center in New York City.

"One day I saw a poster that said, 'Are you Jewish? Do you love to sing? Join the Jewish a capella group.' If I hadn't joined that group, I probably would not have become Orthodox. They met at Hillel House so I started eating my meals there, going to services there led by the

Orthodox rabbi, and finally agreed to have *Shabbos* dinner with the rabbi and his family."

As I listened to Shulamit,who was worldly yet *frum*, religiously observant, I felt my identity resettle. The more I thought about it, I realized that it was okay to play my part in Yehuda's world, and in Chaim's world too. That did not diminish who I was; it just made me a better me.

Toward the end of December, Chaim called to tell us that he and Shulamit were planning to visit us for a day or two so they could go skiing during her winter break from teaching sixth grade at a New York City elementary school. Shulamit had once taken a few lessons but hadn't been on skis for a very long time. Chaim wanted her to try it again. What surprised me was not that they wanted to go skiing but that they were going to sleep under the same roof. They weren't even officially engaged. Penina and Yehuda had not stayed with us until after they were married. But Penina grew up in the *frum* world. Chaim and Shulamit didn't. Then again, after Peter and I became engaged, there were a few times that he and I stayed with his parents at their house while my parents were out of town. So who was I to judge what Chaim and Shulamit chose to do or not to do? As it turned out, Chaim slept in his old room; Shulamit slept in Yehuda's.

Like Penina, Shulamit wore a skirt over her ski pants and asked for a female instructor. After the lesson, she agreed to leave the bunny slope and take the chair lift with Chaim to the top of the beginner slope. But having not yet learned to turn without falling meant the one run she made from the top of the beginner slope was her last.

Shulamit made her parents sound like people Peter and I would enjoy. Just as we had eased ourselves into the role of parents of Orthodox children, they had done the same. Her mother was an art therapist. Her father had retired from teaching computer science, graduated from clown school, and performed in the children's wing of a local hospital. Shulamit told us her parents were fairly laid back. Although I had no preconceived notions as to how they would look, the one thing

I did not expect was the somewhat informal attire Shulamit's parents wore when we first met them.

Leo and Helen had the aura of former hippies. He was in cargo pants and a short-sleeved shirt. She had on a simple green skirt and top. Although I've colored my grey for the past twenty years, Helen did nothing of the sort. She wore her grey hair proudly coiled into a braid behind her head. Our evening together at a kosher restaurant in the city was like being with old friends. We laughed, talked, and laughed some more. Shulamit and Chaim seemed to have as much fun as we parents did. Peter and I looked forward to spending more time with Leo and Helen. But that was up to Chaim and Shulamit. Despite the restrictions of *shomer negiah*—which prohibits contact between members of the opposite sex who are not married to each other—Peter and I shook hands with Leo and Helen as soon as we were introduced, a natural way to greet people in our secular world. And when it was time to say good-bye, we hugged. So as to not offend any of the Orthodox patrons of the restaurant, we waited until we were out on the sidewalk. But I hugged Leo. Peter hugged Helen. If we embarrassed Chaim or Shulamit, they never brought it up. I hugged Leo.

After dating Shulamit for two months, Chaim talked with me about engagement rings. He wanted to give her something special but did not have a lot of money to spend. He was only three when Nana died but he remembered her as "a nice lady who had great toys to play with—especially a plastic lawnmower that she kept in her closet." Shulamit made him so very, very happy so I offered him Nana's diamond. I wanted her to have it.

"I can't," he said, waving me off. "It reminds you of Nana."

"She would have been so proud of your dedication to Judaism," I said, tearfully.

During the next few weeks, Chaim and Shulamit made the rounds of jewelry stores, hoping to find a setting they both liked and that he could afford. Chaim cautioned me to not say anything to Shulamit about the "r" word (ring), the "w" word (wedding), or the "m" word (marriage) until he gave me the "all clear." Though deeply in love with

Shulamit, he was uncomfortable that several members of her family were married to non-Jews. He needed time to work this out.

One sunny afternoon in February, four months after they first met, Chaim showed up at Shulamit's apartment with four bouquets of roses; brought her to a park at the top of Manhattan; serenaded her with his own romantic version of her favorite song; bent down on his knee; and asked her to marry him.

When their engagement party was in its planning stage, Chaim called me with a list of caterers that he wanted me to check out; because I had gone through Yehuda's wedding, I knew about kosher caterers in the city

"Sorry," I told Chaim, "None of them fit in our budget."

"Yehuda and Penina had a nice party," he said. "Don't we deserve one?"

"Of course, but . . ."

"All you want is the cheapest party possible."

We each have our own ways of coping with stress. Of course, Chaim wanted to have a great engagement party. But there were limits. Was this sibling rivalry? *Was something missing from Chaim's childhood that he wanted us to make up for? Was he trying to impress Shulamit?*

"Have you heard of the commandment to honor your father and mother?" I said, angrily.

After a long pause Chaim said, "You're right, Mom. Sorry to be such a pain."

"All Dad and I want is for you and Shulamit to be happy. Don't you know that?"

"I guess so."

Chaim seemed to have mellowed by the time he came up to spend a day skiing with us. Content was the way to describe him. I was washing mustard off my hands after making cheese sandwiches to take for lunch when he came into the kitchen. He was smiling. A small box was in his hand.

"Hope you like what I did," he said, handing me the box.

"What's this?" I asked.

"Open it and see."

Wrapped in layers of tissue paper was my ring. Chaim had re-placed the diamond with a sapphire, my favorite gemstone. I was so thrilled he had thought of me in the midst of planning his wedding that I could think of nothing to say but "Thanks."

"Put it on," he suggested.

So I did.

It was Chaim's idea to hold the engagement party downstairs in his apartment building. Peter and I helped Leo and Helen shop for the bagels, the spreads, the salads, and a Carvel cake (Shulamit's favorite). Despite the casual surroundings, we dressed up. With no separate seat-ing for men and women, I felt at ease, instead of left out.

At one point, Chaim asked for quiet so that he could complete the chapter he was studying in the *Talmud*. (The tradition of publicly com-pleting a unit of study is called a *siyum* and is usually followed by a celebration.) In the midst of celebrating his engagement, Chaim thought it only fitting that he have a *siyum*. His rabbi was highly impressed.

On the way to the ski area, Peter and Chaim had tossed around ideas as to what Chaim should wear to his wedding.

"Dad wore a morning suit to ours because that's what my mother picked out," I said. "Yehuda wore a black suit to his because that's what he always wears on special occasions. By the way, doesn't the groom usually stay out of the wedding plans?"

"Shulamit's not comfortable making all the decisions," Chaim said, "If I do stuff with her, it becomes an adventure."

Chaim wanted an outdoor ceremony. Shulamit wanted men and women to sit together during the ceremony and the reception. They both wanted a large dance floor with a *mechitza* so that men and women would dance separately. Helen and I were given the job of help-ing them find the place to hold it. Located somewhere in Brooklyn, Chaya's Terrace seemed to hold the most promise.

One morning, I took the train to New York and the subway to Brooklyn where Helen picked me up, and we hugged like old friends.

"The guy who answered the phone made me feel as if I was or-dering a pizza," Helen told me. "He gave me a price that sounded reasonable if we have a minimum of 450 people, and a price per person if we have less. I did the math. Turns out to cost the same per person no matter how many people."

After a tour of the catering hall, we were both impressed. Elaborately decorated without being ornate, it had an outdoor gazebo for the ceremony, ballrooms with large areas for dancing, and mixed seating was allowed.

Over salads at a nearby dairy restaurant, we raised our water glasses and toasted our good luck. After lunch, I called Chaim.

"It has everything you and Shulamit asked for," I told him.

"We'll check it out one night when it's set up for a *simcha* (a celebration)."

True to his word, he brought Shulamit to see it a few nights later. After a quick tour, he called to say it was not right for them.

"No more mixed seating," he told me. "The neighbors complained."

"What do they have to do with it?" I asked.

"Beats me."

"Any chance Shulamit will consider separate seating?"

"Can't do that to her family. Even the sound of separate seating might set some people off."

29

Why Would Anyone Do That to a Duck?

Chaim and Shulamit chose the Huntington Town House on Long Island for their wedding. My brother's *bar mitzvah* party was held there many years before, so the experience of the flaming duck was still fresh in my mind. Let me explain. The movie *The Bridge on the River Kwai* came out the same year as my brother's *bar mitzvah*. Once the guests were seated for the celebration in honor of my brother, the ballroom lights dimmed, the band played the theme song from the movie, and the waiters marched across the ballroom carrying swords of flaming duck. Despite the "oohs" and "aahs" from the invited guests, I thought it was awful!

"Think they'll do the thing with the ducks?" Chaim asked me. "I'd love to see it."

"I didn't know you and Shulamit are into duck," I said.

"Thought it would be fun."

Seemed like a waste of money to me. But it was their wedding.

When Chaim checked with the Huntington Town House, he was disappointed to find out that they no longer did the flaming duck.

30

Not Even a Little Off-Color

Shopping for clothes is sometimes better done alone, as was the case when I searched for a dress for Yehuda's wedding. Wanting to wear something different the second time around, I took a chance on visiting dress shops with Shulamit and her mother in Brooklyn, the land of Orthodox weddings.

Shulamit didn't intend to micromanage her own wedding but wanted it to be "picture perfect." Not the type who spent hours pouring over issue after issue of brides' magazines, she preferred the person-to-person approach. Did I know of any reason why the floral centerpieces had to match the bridesmaid's bouquets, as the florist insisted? There was no way to tell whether Shulamit sought my advice out of politeness or indecision. But I liked being asked.

"Whatever feels right to you is the way to go," I told her.

"Thanks, Mom," Shulamit said, giving me a big hug. "I was hoping you'd say that."

Helen had reserved a slot at a fancy dress shop on one of the main shopping streets, so I suggested she go first. One gown looked great, but the full skirt made her feel like Cinderella.

The gowns at the next place were so ugly that Shulamit and I had no choice but to giggle.

The next shop looked promising. The first gown I tried on was perfect—a sleeveless sheath that fell to my mid-calf and a matching jacket, in ecru, with just a hint of light green, and trimmed with pearls. A far different look than what I wore to Yehuda's wedding.

31

A Fall Without Curls

Shulamit made an appointment with a *sheitel macher* in Brooklyn and invited Helen and me to come along. Once again I took an early train and the subway to Brooklyn. The stop at New Utrecht Avenue began to feel like home. On the way, I thought back to the fun I had shopping with Shulamit for candlesticks a few weeks before.

The *sheitel* shop was on the third floor of a building that also housed a tattoo parlor and a waxing and tanning salon. Helen was waiting for us when we walked in the door. Shulamit wanted a *sheitel* in the same color and length as her own hair, but without curls. So the stylist took down the longer wigs—displayed on Styrofoam heads around the tiny salon—and positioned them on Shulamit, who made her selection in no time at all.

With the stylist's permission, Helen and I tried on some of the shorter *sheitels* that were on display. Our heads were not cut out for *sheitels*, we both decided, but Shulamit took our picture anyway. I still look at it whenever I need a good laugh.

32

Pretty in Pink

Instead of insisting that her bridesmaids wear matching gowns, Shulamit asked them each to put together an ensemble of their own choosing. It just had to be pink. Though they each owned either a jacket, blouse, skirt or dress in the appropriate color, finding the rest of the ensemble wasn't easy, because pink was not the "in" color that year. One friend wondered whether her pink sleeveless dress would still fit; another worried that the jacket to her pink suit might have to be taken in and would no longer look good with the matching skirt; and so on. Even Penina called Shulamit from Israel to ask her to rethink her color request.

Somehow, on the day of the wedding, each bridesmaid was perfectly decked out in pink.

33

The Story of the Dog and the Guinea Pig

The week before Chaim's wedding was not what Peter and I expected. Having already chartered a bus for Sunday to transport our friends to Long Island for the wedding, rented the movie *Crossing Delancey* for the trip, and stuffed the party bags with kosher snacks for the trip, we both thought we were pretty well-prepared.

On Monday, someone asked if he could bring his dog on the bus for the ride home.

"Not a good idea," Peter told him.

"What if I check with the bus company?"

"Not everyone likes dogs," Peter said, trying to be tactful.

"But he's hypo-allergenic."

This friend was not getting the message that his dog wasn't an invited guest, so Peter finally told him there was no room left on the bus.

On Tuesday, someone else asked if we minded transporting her daughter's guinea pig in its cage on the bus. Her daughter hoped that one of our guests would fall in love and would want to adopt it.

"Sorry," I said, "No room left on the bus."

What was it with our friends and their pets? Didn't they realize we were planning a wedding, not a pet show?

34

Trying to Stay Dry in Deep Water

On the Wednesday before his wedding, Peter and I had a great time with Chaim. But helping make room for Shulamit in his apartment took longer than expected, so we didn't get to bed until late that night. Yehuda and his family were arriving from Israel the next morning and agreed to call us as soon as they got to Penina's parents' house. Chaim's wedding was enough to keep me up. No sooner did I finally fall asleep than I woke up waiting for Yehuda's phone call.

I enjoyed myself on Thursday preparing oven-baked salmon, a tossed salad, a mixed bean salad, and marinated cucumbers, in addition to an extra-large apple crisp with a double layer of crunch on top—all per Chaim's request—for the *Shabbos* dinner that Chaim, Yehuda, Peter and I would enjoy together at Chaim's apartment on Friday evening.

Peter and I were out the door early on Friday, having loaded the car the night before. Peter had packed a tuxedo for the wedding, a suit for the *aufruf*, and a navy blue blazer and black pants for the *sheva brachot*. My bag was filled with my gown for the wedding, a turquoise linen suit with a scalloped skirt for the *aufruf*, and the navy one with white lapels that I had worn to Yehuda's *sheva brachot*, five years before, and would also wear to Chaim's.

When I think back to that Friday night at Chaim's apartment, I remember how good it felt to be a family of four again, even if for only a little while. I had no desire to go back in time to when Yehuda and Chaim were young. I was happy with both of them as Orthodox men—one who already had a wife and a family, the other who was about to be married. That evening there was no sibling rivalry. There were no disagreements at all. But there was a lot of laughter and love.

Chaim's *aufruf* was at the synagogue that sponsored the luncheon where he and Shulamit first met. Just as Penina had not gone to Yehuda's *aufruf*, Shulamit would not be at Chaim's. The bride and groom weren't supposed to be in touch the week prior to their wedding. If something important came up, messages were to be transmitted by a third party. Chaim had acted as Yehuda's *shomer*. Yehuda did the same for Chaim.

I felt just as alone in the women's section of the synagogue during Chaim's *aufruf* as I had during Yehuda's. The other women smiled greetings, but I still missed my family on the other side of the *mechitza*. Following the service, there was a *Kiddush* in Chaim's honor. Walking back to Chaim's apartment, Peter and I lagged behind so our sons could talk. It was so rare that Yehuda found the need to praise his younger brother that we decided to let them have some time to themselves.

Yehuda stayed with Chaim again that evening. Peter and I walked back to our hotel.

At 8:30 a.m. on Sunday, we spoke to Yehuda. Chaim wasn't even awake. Peter and I had hoped to get to the catering hall early, but first we had to pick up Penina and our three granddaughters in Brooklyn and drive them to a hotel near the catering hall where we would all spend the night. Our rooms weren't ready when we got to the hotel, so we had to wait.

When we finally arrived at the catering hall, the photographer was getting ready to start. Our two and one-half, one and one-half, and six-month-old granddaughters were still in play clothes. Penina and I hoped for a touchup from the makeup artist, but she had already left. Peter rushed off to find Chaim. Yehuda was nowhere in sight.

I finally felt put together when someone brought me to the Chassan's *Tish*, the groom's reception room. Chaim, Yehuda, Peter, Leo, and Chaim's rabbi were seated at a table. Bottles of schnapps and paper cups were lined up in front of them.

Helen was beautiful in a butter-on-butter colored satin suit and matching hat with ribbon and appliqué. Leaning in for a hug, we almost lost our wide-brimmed hats.

Chaim's rabbi placed the plain white plate that Chaim had asked me to buy into the white silk bag that Helen had hand-sewn. He pulled out a chair and gestured for us to break the plate. But the plastic chair was too soft to break the plate. So someone handed us a hammer; one whack and that was it for the plate.

Helen and I found Shulamit in the bride's dressing room. She looked stunning; her brilliant black hair beautifully coiffed into soft curls that gently framed her face and fell past her shoulders; her gown of white empire satin with a mandarin collar and a full skirt, with curlicues of embroidered beading on the bodice was exquisite.

Later at the *bedeckin*, as Chaim lifted Shulamit's veil and placed it over her face, I felt their love fill the air.

The wedding ceremony took place outside under a *chupah* draped with daisies and roses. Other than that, it was the same as Yehuda's.

There was mixed seating for dinner, but the dance floor was split by a *mechitza*. Someone whisked me into the center of the room with Shulamit and Helen. A circle formed around us as we whirled around. Within moments, Penina and Malka took my hands and were joined by many of my friends. I have no idea how long we danced but I was winded way before I sat back down.

The evening flew. I had a great time.

35

The Singularity of One

Penina and Yehuda went to Israel during their second year of marriage. Chaim and Shulamit went early in their first. Maybe Shulamit was ready to take time off from teaching. Or Chaim wanted a break before his second year of doctoral study. No matter, a month after their wedding, Chaim and Shulamit placed their belongings in a self-storage unit and left for Israel. Their apartment on the West Bank came furnished, but some of the furniture was falling apart. Chaim liked being within walking distance of the *yeshiva*. Though Shulamit put up with the long ride on the bulletproof bus to her seminary – something like a female version of a *yeshiva* – in Jerusalem, she hitched a ride happily whenever someone from the community was going in that direction. A full year in Israel had been their intent, but Shulamit wanted to give birth in the States, so they came back early and settled in metropolitan New York.

My mother was okay with Yehuda and Penina having three children—not as if they needed her permission—but after they had Freidl, she couldn't contain herself.

"When is your son going to leave his wife alone?" my mother had the nerve to ask me. "Doesn't he know the facts of life? All she needs is another baby! It's your job to tell him enough is enough."

"They are adults," I said, enunciating every syllable. "The number of children they have is not up to you or me."

"If they keep having kids, they'll never be able to keep up with their bills."

"They're happy," I said, emphasizing the word happy, while trying not to lose my cool.

A child of the 60s, I had given little thought to having grandchildren. Little did I realize "Perfect love does not come until the first grandchild" is not only a Welsch proverb, but also an absolute fact. Each grandchild is as precious as the next. Being a grandmother is one of the best jobs in the world.

A month after Penina gave birth to Freidl, Shulamit gave birth to our first grandson. Helen and Leo were at the hospital when we arrived. How wonderful to share a grandchild with them! Shulamit and Chaim were euphoric but needed sleep. So Peter and Leo drove Chaim home to get some rest while Helen and I stayed with Shulamit and took turns cuddling our new grandson so she could rest.

Bris Milah, the ritual circumcision done eight days after a Jewish baby boy's birth, is the commandment most commonly observed, even by secular Jews. More than a simple medical procedure, the *bris* is a religious ceremony that signifies the covenant between God and the Jews. It is performed by a *mohel*, a pious Jew trained in the physical procedures of circumcision.

Avraham's *bris* took place at the synagogue where Chaim and Shulamit first met. The *bris* is a rite of passage for the baby, but is often an emotional experience for the mother. And Shulamit was no exception. The ceremony was in the main sanctuary. We adjourned to another room for the celebration. Since I was dressed in the same clothes I wore in Israel, it felt strange to be at a baby party where people spoke English.

The next day Peter and I left for Israel so we could get to know Freidl.

36

No Bugs Allowed

In 2006, the year after Chaim and Shulamit were married, Penina and Yehuda came back to the States for a visit. Peter and I worked hard to establish a relationship with our grandchildren. Visiting them in Israel at least four times a year was one way we maintained it. Penina and Yehuda understood that so much traveling was taking its toll on us. So staying with us for the first part of their visit was their way of thanking us for making the effort.

Initially, I was overjoyed. Then unease set in. We had grown accustomed to having the house to ourselves, relatively free from noise or commotion. Chaim and Shulamit had one child. Yehuda and Penina had four. Whew! With Peter and me, that added up to eleven of us.

Were there enough places for everyone to sleep? Peter and I had our own bed. Yehuda and Penina could have the high riser in the guest room. Freidl, their infant daughter, would be with them in the portable crib from when they lived in Beacon Hills and had only one child. Four-year-old Liba and three-year-old Eva would sleep on mattresses placed on the floor in Yehuda's old room. We would need to buy a porta-crib for Blimi, who was almost two. Chaim and Shulamit would have Chaim's old room and would bring their own porta-crib for Avraham.

Peter told me not to fixate on the food, insisting that everyone would eat whatever I cooked. He sounded so confident. But I am a mother who likes to nurture. Providing my family with food they enjoy makes me happy. With no kosher restaurants in our area, there would be no eating out. Everyone but Peter loved soup, so I froze one gallon of potato-leek soup (Penina's recipe) and another of vegetable bean soup (my own recipe). Both could be served with either meat or dairy meals. Chaim and Yehuda used to love my meatballs and spaghetti, so I pre-cooked two pounds of meatballs and froze them. Salmon was always a winner. After preparing and freezing three pounds of oven-baked salmon, I had no desire to fry chicken cutlets for *Shabbos*. Chaim said we could buy them already cooked at one of the kosher supermarkets in his neighborhood the next time we visited.

Peter leased a fourteen-passenger van with three car seats and one infant seat. Chaim and Shulamit drove their own car. What a wonderful surprise when they met us at the airport. Tears of joy dripped down my cheeks as I watched Chaim and Yehuda embrace. Hard to believe that a head of lettuce might cause tension between them.

The problem was that we Jews aren't supposed to eat bugs of any sort. No chocolate-covered ants. No sun-dried spiders. Not even toasted tarantulas. Having never gone in search of bugs to eat, I may, nonetheless, have been eating them unwittingly for most of my life, probably even feeding them to my family. I used to take Yehuda and Chaim berry picking at nearby farms. Strawberries. Raspberries. Yum! We pulled the berries off the plants and popped them into our mouths. Sometimes we pried the green stem off the strawberries, sometimes not. Who cared if our fingers turned red or if we dripped berry juice on our clothes? That was part of the fun. We undoubtedly ate a lot more berries than we put in our baskets. Who knew that tucked inside those tasty berries lurked the possibility of bugs?

Most of the places we went picking are now housing developments. And picking is not as much fun without kids to help. So I go to the local farmstand instead. If I close my eyes, their berries taste almost as sweet as the ones we used to pick. But now that Yehuda and Chaim are Orthodox, I had to learn to wash berries in a new way. First I cut off the top quarter of the berry in order to see down into the inner white core, checking for any trace of bugs. Then the berries have to soak in the same special fruit-and-vegetable wash that Chaim asked me to use for lettuce.

It surprised me that Yehuda gave up fresh strawberries in favor of frozen ones that came already inspected for bugs and bearing the special seal of approval from the kosher supervisory group that meets his standards. What was the big deal if he ate a tiny fragment of a bug? The problem is that bugs are verboten according to the laws of kashruth. And the last thing I wanted was to argue with him about bugs.

Food is the language of motherhood. So one night I made a luscious salad with locally grown produce but used the lettuce that came labeled triple-washed and inspected by the appropriate kosher supervisory group. Locally grown lettuce was fine for Chaim as long as it was soaked in the special solution. Even the triple-washed lettuce had to be soaked in that stuff before he would allow his family to eat it. Much to my dismay, after Yehuda learned that the lettuce in the salad was grown in soil, he asked his family not to eat any salad. I was hurt. I had done my best, only to have Yehuda insinuate that it was not good enough. Instead of making a scene in front of the grandchildren, I placed the salad in front of Peter and silently walked back to the kitchen. It took me some time to calm down. Wanting to provide Yehuda's family with a vegetable to go along with their meal, I searched the freezer, found some green beans, and threw them into a pot of boiling water.

Once the grandchildren were in bed, I pulled Yehuda aside and asked him, as calmly as I could, "What was wrong with the lettuce?"

"Sorry," he said. "But no amount of washing is going to make soil-grown lettuce completely bug-free." Putting his arms around me, he added, "But I really appreciate you doing everything you can to make me happy."

With that experience in mind the next time they came, I bought the same kind of hydroponic lettuce grown in Israel that I thought Penina used. (Lettuce grown in water is considered to be bug-free.) I was able to buy it at a kosher supermarket in Monsey a few hours drive from our home. Opening the package I tried to convince myself that whether or not Yehuda ate the lettuce was of no importance. What was important was that we were all together. One family.

Noticing the big bag of hydroponic lettuce on the kitchen counter, Yehuda thanked me profusely but added, "Sorry we won't be eating it. Of the two hydroponic farms in Israel, this one is under investigation for improper supervision of their produce."

"If you don't want to eat it, you don't have to," I said, trying to hide my disappointment. "I'm going to serve it anyway."

Though Chaim's brand of Orthodoxy was easier to take, it bothered me that he was often unyielding when it came to accepting Yehuda's right to his own beliefs.

At dinner, after watching the salad bowl pass from one end of the table to the other, Chaim asked his brother, "Got a problem with the salad?" Yehuda looked at his empty salad bowl and did not reply. "Not good enough for you?" Chaim went on, sounding ready for a fight.

"Great dinner, Mom," Shulamit said before Chaim could get another word out. "What's for dessert?"

Later that evening I pulled Chaim aside.

"Yehuda's a big boy," I said. "What's right for you doesn't have to be right for him."

I try hard not to fixate on this bug thing, but every so often it creeps up on me. In honor of our third annual family gathering, I made a pot of soup, the kind my sons both love, hearty vegetable with basil, parsley, and oregano. But I added spinach.

When Yehuda came down for breakfast the first morning, he decided that cold soup would be a good start. Taking the big metal pot from the refrigerator and placing it on the counter, he told me how wonderful it smelled. But after lifting the cover, ladle in hand, he looked so disappointed.

"Mom, there's spinach in the soup," he said.

"There sure is," I said, proudly, "I opened a special can of Star-K spinach."

The year before, I might have been angry. But now it did not bother me. If there's a harder way to approach a given situation, Yehuda is likely to follow it. He's intense, like me.

The next morning I made another batch of the same soup, minus the spinach.

37

A Hard Way to Fall Asleep

A lot of planning preceded our second family gathering a year later. Eleven of us were going to be together again for almost two weeks. Some time before, Yehuda had called to say that he felt really close to us and that he always wanted to feel comfortable having his family stay in our home. Hearing those words made me so happy that I was probably still repeating them in my head and hearing only half of what came next. I think Yehuda may have said he did not want us to watch TV or use the Internet while his family was here, but after hearing Peter said that was okay with him, I said it was fine with me. I didn't think Yehuda would enforce his request, and even if he did, how bad could it be? But as he went on to tell us that to ensure our compliance, he planned to sever the connection between our home and the cable service, I felt my stomach tighten. This was going too far. Of the three TVs in our house, the one in our bedroom keeps me company on nights when I cannot sleep. On the previous visit, Yehuda had asked us not to watch television on *Shabbos* so I had turned down the volume and looked at the pictures.

After Yehuda hung up, I complained to Peter, "No TV for a week is too much to ask!"

"Don't worry," Peter said, "I'll take care of the one in our bedroom."

But he never did.

Mister Rogers' Neighborhood was one of the few television shows I let our sons watch when they were youngsters. It's doubtful that any of our grandchildren will have the opportunity to see quality programs like that because neither Yehuda nor Chaim owns a TV. Mindful of the sex and violence possible at any hour of the day and hoping to shelter his children from the realities of the outside world, Yehuda doesn't even want them to know that television exists. Is it possible to live a full life without ever watching TV? Of course. Would it be possible to find appropriate programs for our grandchildren to watch? Absolutely. But I'd never do that unless I had the parents' permission. Chaim never owned a television; Shulamit did when she was single. She also had a VCR and a DVD player. But after they were married, Chaim asked her to give it all away. Addicted to what he called "junk TV" whenever he visited us, he stayed up until three or four o'clock in the morning watching reruns of the *The Dukes of Hazard* or *Tic Tac Do* or *The Price is Right* or *The Bachelor*. The only way to kick his habit was to avoid having a TV in his home. Shulamit wasn't happy about parting with her TV but gave it up out of love for Chaim.

As Conservative Jews, Peter and I fit somewhere between the progressive attitude of the Reform and the strictness of the Orthodox. Yehuda and Chaim believe that the *Torah* is of Divine origin. Their wives wear *sheitels*. Their homes are strictly kosher. Yehuda is ultra-Orthodox. Chaim is more modern Orthodox. Their main areas of disagreement are three. First of all is the degree to which they engage or disengage with secular society. Yehuda lives in a strictly Orthodox suburb of Jerusalem. Chaim's home is in a mixed neighborhood in a suburb of New York. Second is the weight they assign to *Torah* study as compared to secular studies. Yehuda downplays the fact that he has a college degree. For him the study of *Torah* is a full-time job. Chaim studies *Torah* in his spare time. His full-time job is in the field of biology. He's very happy with his life the way it is, but did tell me that after his children are grown, he would love to dedicate himself to full-time *Talmudic* studies. Peter never misses a chance to tell Yehuda to get "a real job," but is finally beginning to accept him as an adult. Though we never set out to raise a *Talmudic* scholar, that doesn't mean there's anything wrong with Yehuda turning out that way. And finally there is the level of importance they attach to *chumras*, stringencies in the interpretation of Jewish law. Yehuda adheres to all of them. Chaim feels they are open to interpretation.

People ask why I always did as Yehuda asked. In truth, I didn't. In the beginning, I felt as if Yehuda was insinuating that I was not Jewish enough. What was wrong with the food in my pantry? Nothing contained ingredients that were clearly not kosher. And I cooked only dairy in my dairy pots and meat in the meat pots. So why did everything have to be immersed in the *mikvah*? And what about bugs? It took time for me to realize that what I have is what I hoped for. Starting when our boys were toddlers, I told them that being Jewish was special, something of which they should be proud. But not being allowed to watch TV in the privacy of my own bedroom was not an accommodation. It was an outright imposition.

Having refused us access to the Internet, Yehuda gave in to Chaim who needed access via his laptop for his graduate studies. So one night after the grandkids were in bed for several hours, I asked Chaim for help in accessing my e-mail on his computer. Was I wrong to go against Yehuda's wishes? Maybe. But only minutes before, Peter had done the same thing, without being caught by Yehuda. So I thought I was safe. Then I looked up and saw Yehuda walking stiffly through the archway that led from the kitchen to my workspace.

"I thought we had an agreement," Yehuda said, his tone a mixture of irritation and disappointment. "No Internet and no TV while we're here!"

Who was the parent here? Part of me wanted to ream him out for being so rigid. The other part reminded me he was not going to change.

"My girls are diamonds," Yehuda said, leering at Chaim. "I'll do whatever it takes to protect them."

"Who made you boss?" Chaim asked, inching forward a foot or so, his voice getting louder with each word.

I stepped between them.

Yehuda turned and silently walked away.

Every so often I find myself in an untenable position, sacrificing my need to be "in the right" for the sake of maintaining family harmony. There were eight more days of togetherness. A resurrection of brotherly resentment was the last thing anyone needed. Yehuda was doing the best he knew to take care of his family. Would I have acted differently in his shoes? Maybe not.

Sighing deeply, my hands resting on Chaim's shoulders I said, "I shouldn't have put you in the middle."

"It's your house!" Chaim told me.

"Do me a favor and pretend this never happened with Yehuda."

A long moment later, Chaim said he would try.

Gingerly making my way to the sunroom off the kitchen where Yehuda was talking softly with Penina, I got ready to humble myself, something I hate to do. But at 11:00 p.m., exhausted from frustration and lack of sleep, humility was easier than confrontation. I did not want to apologize, but what other choice was there? After listening to my apology, Yehuda put his arms around me, thanked me, and told me that he loved me. Pretty soon, I found myself upstairs. My bed beckoned, but I was too worked up for sleep. Television wasn't an option, so I cleaned out my closet for an hour and then fell into a sound sleep.

By morning, things had settled down considerably. Chaim and Yehuda were *davening* next to each other in the sunroom. Although Penina had sat silently—but teary-eyed—and watched me apologize to Yehuda, now she was all smiles. As soon as I walked into the kitchen, she gave me a warm hug.

"I love you, Mom," she said.

"I love you, too," I said, returning her embrace.

38

Being Fruitful

I was stupefied upon learning that Penina's aunt has twelve children. Hard to remember who told me or when I first found out. My parents have two children, as do Peter's parents, Peter and I, and the majority of our friends. But Yehuda and Penina already had five children under the age of six within the first six years of their marriage. This discomfited me until I started to look at things from a different perspective. Yehuda's religious transformation may have had a deeper effect on me than I realized.

Do the Orthodox believe in birth control? That was the sort of question I was uncomfortable asking Yehuda. So I asked the wife of one of his friends who, at that point, had already given birth to seven children. Was I being inappropriate in asking her this question, I wondered. She had already told me to help myself to anything I might want to eat in her refrigerator. So I decided to take a chance. Thinking back I can't believe I was so bold. Most Orthodox are private people. Birth control is not the type of subject I usually brought up with someone I didn't really know, but there was no one else to ask.

I already knew that before a Jewish couple gets married they go through genetic testing to ensure that neither of them is a carrier of Tay-Sachs disease or any other inherited disorders—Peter and I once went through those tests. It seems that most Orthodox couples wait until they have at least one boy and one girl before they even consider birth control, unless there's a problem with one of the existing children that takes too much time for the mother to tend to. Before birth control is considered, the couple first consults with their rabbi. After asking them a few questions—I was not comfortable asking exactly what questions these might be—the rabbi gives the couple various options to consider. Birth control is often one of these options. Basically that was all I was able to find out. Yehuda's friend's wife didn't seem to want to tell me anything more on the topic.

I used to ask people how many children they have until I learned that in the Orthodox world many women who are barren feel as though they've sinned.

The *Torah* states: "And God blessed them and said to them, 'Be fruitful and multiply; fill the earth and subdue it." (Genesis 1:28). Over the years this has been interpreted to mean that every Jewish man should father at least one boy and one girl. And yet, although many Orthodox couples may believe that God does the family planning and that birth control is not a necessity, *Halacha*, Jewish law, does permit birth control in certain circumstances: if the couple already has a girl and a boy; if the woman is very young or is nursing an infant; or if pregnancy poses a risk to the mother's life.

The documentary *Be Fruitful and Multiply* was recently presented before a mostly secular Jewish audience at our local Jewish Community Center. It was billed as a portrait of ultra-Orthodox women in Brooklyn and Israel discussing the joys and pressures of having large families. I would have liked Peter to go with me, but he was on a ski trip with his buddies. So I tagged along with a friend and her husband. I was excited about seeing the movie in the hope of learning more about the Orthodox. My expectation was that it would put a positive spin on large families. But by the time the lights came back on, I felt as if a trust had been violated.

At first the mothers spoke rather matter-of-factly about the amount of work and time involved in raising a lot of children. But I couldn't help cringing as the movie progressed. The filmmaker asked a mother of fourteen children if she knew all their names. *What a stupid question!* Did she expect the mother to say that they wear name tags? I could hardly believe the mother was obliging enough to recite all the names.

As the interview progressed, the topic got around to *Shabbos* preparation. The children proudly described their duties. The older ones had jobs like baking *challah*, cooking the *cholent*, making the salad or washing the kitchen floor. One set the table. And so on. It was rewarding to see how eager they were to follow through on their responsibilities. Was it my imagination or did someone in the audience yell out, "Child labor?" I turned to see if I could make out the heckler but the auditorium was too dark. What would he say about my five-year-old granddaughter whose skill in using a paring knife results in paper-thin slices of zucchini? What about her three-year-old sister who knows the recipe for the apple *kugel* that she "helps" make by flipping the switch on the food processor? How about their four-year-old sister who carries a glass bottle of wine to the table every Friday night without ever dropping it?

One woman in the movie had heavy-duty feelings against large families. She told of the trauma of having so many siblings that she was forced to sleep in a neighbor's home. *At least she had a place to sleep. She felt neglected by her mother.* Bad parents are everywhere. She said the worst thing a parent could do to a child was have a lot of children. Yet in the middle of her tirade against big families, she talked about how much she loved her job as a labor coach who helped women give birth. *Talk about cognitive dissonance!*

Once the movie was over, there was a question-and-answer session with two prominent local Jewish women. One was a social worker. The other was the wife of an Orthodox rabbi and the mother of thirteen children.

I raised my hand first.

"I feel sorry for the birthing coach," I said. "She was so sad. That her own mother ignored her was awful. There are bad parents everywhere. But my daughter-in-law has five children. And she takes time out for each of them."

As I sat back down, a large portion of the audience behind me booed me. *How dare they?* My spine stiffened. I had a mind to smack every single one of them. I was about to storm to the back of the auditorium when I realized there are stupid people everywhere; my feeding into their ignorance would serve no purpose but theirs.

Someone asked the rabbi's wife what gave her the right to have so many children at a time when the environment was being depleted at a rapid rate. *That woman is an idiot! Did she think we were living in China? I wanted to tell her to go home and plant a vegetable garden.*

"I do my best to recycle," said the rabbi's wife. " And who's to say that one of my thirteen children isn't going to grow up and come up with a way to solve the depletion of the environment?"

Next was an elderly looking man who needed help getting to his feet.

"Don't you all realize how important it is to replenish the Jewish population of the world?" he asked. "What with the Holocaust and intermarriage, there seem to be less of us every year."

It surprised me that he wasn't booed for bringing up intermarriage, a sore point in most of the Jewish world. Maybe the mention of the Holocaust was enough to keep the loud mouths shut.

The next to speak was a man who said his grandmother gave birth at least twelve times.

"What with infant mortality rates," he said, "You just had to have a lot of kids to run the family farm."

In the coatroom, I came across this man and told him I appreciated what he had said.

"I just told it as it was," he said

"Wasn't that awful?" his wife asked me. "I can't believe they booed you. People are so rude!" She went on to tell me that although she has no child of her own, she does have a stepchild from her husband's first marriage. "People I barely know come up to me and ask why I don't have another."

"That's none of their business," I told her.

Two weeks after the showing of *Be Fruitful and Multiply*, it still bothered me. It was not just a movie. It was a putdown of my son's way of life. I still don't understand why anyone would want a large family. But I definitely don't begrudge them their choice.

39

Mother Tongue

Some time ago, I attended a lecture on the life of Irving Berlin, the Jewish composer who wrote the score for *White Christmas* among other movies. Although the event took place at the Reform synagogue in a nearby town, it was part of an ongoing series of monthly presentations sponsored by the Jewish Federation and open to all Jewish seniors. Though I'm usually one of the youngest in attendance, I try to make at least one or two per year. It's a great way to commune with another sector of the Jewish community.

As I was leaving, the woman in charge of the lecture series approached me and asked if I'd consider being part of an upcoming panel discussion on the pleasures and challenges of having a child move to Israel. I knew who she was, but we'd never been introduced.

"How do you know I have a child in Israel?" I asked her.

"Word gets around," she said.

I took that in and then said, "If I'm not visiting the grandkids in Israel the day of the panel discussion, I'd be happy to take part."

After we exchanged phone numbers, she said she'd call me when the details were finalized.

I could not see talking about having a child living in Israel without addressing Yehuda's religious transformation. Yet after the fiasco at the JCC, I realized the possible implications of addressing another audience comprised primarily of Reform and Conservative Jews. My wound was still fresh from being booed during the question-and-answer session after the documentary.

Then I started thinking about a conversation that took place when Yehuda was first becoming observant. When the phone rang that Sunday afternoon, I thought it was Yehuda saying he had left something in his room. But no, it was my friend Sue.

"Is he gone yet?" Sue asked. Her manner startled me.

"You mean Yehuda?" I asked.

"Who else?"

"It was great having him home," I said. "Hasn't done laundry for a month. Still turns the stereo up so loud I'm afraid he'll go deaf. Sill loves my cooking, but had some suggestions for *Shabbos*."

"What about this religion thing?" she asked, sounding exasperated. She's an ultra-Reform Jew. Jewish laws and customs are not high on her list.

I explained that Yehuda's *benching* after dinner reminded me of my grandparents.

"So it's starting already. If you don't watch out, you're going to become Orthodox too!"

"You make it sound as if being Orthodox is a disease."

"Your life is going to be much more difficult than you ever imagined." I had no idea where she was going with this, so I let her rant. "We had these friends who were just as normal as you and me. A few years ago, they changed synagogues, became Orthodox, and gave up skiing."

"I don't see what skiing has to do with being religious. Yehuda loves to ski."

"Be careful," she warned me. "Those Orthodox are different from the rest of us."

What made her an expert?

"There's nothing wrong with being religious," I said, still unsure how I felt about Yehuda's budding religiosity but not about to share this with her. She was coming on way too strong. The last thing I wanted was to buy into her negativity. "Yehuda's very happy with his life."

"How's he look? No short black pants? No long white socks? No big fur hat?"

What was her problem?

"Yehuda's not Hassidic, just Orthodox." I said, my anger starting to rise. "All Hassidic are Orthodox. But not all Orthodox are Hassidic."

"Hassidic? Orthodox? Same difference. You ever see those guys at the Thruway rest stop near Monsey?" She did not wait for an answer. "You've got to admit they look weird in those high socks, short pants, and long coats."

The conversation was getting tiresome, but she did have a point. A large Hassidic community populated Monsey. But what gave her the right to tell others how to dress?

"Those Orthodox are so self-righteous," she continued. "They think they're better than the rest of us."

I was going to remind her about the times she complained to me that her half-Jewish grandchildren were baptized when her doorbell rang and she suddenly hung up.

Every accusation Sue made against the Orthodox was amplified in the sentiments I heard expressed after the documentary at the JCC. Was I crazy to consider being part of the upcoming panel discussion? Though it was hard to tell if some who attended the senior lectures came more out of interest in the free buffet lunch than the presentation, the audience always seemed fairly tame. Then again, anti-Orthodox sentiment is no harder to find in upstate New York than in the rest of the Jewish world.

A long, long time ago all Jews were Orthodox. Jewish laws, teachings, and customs once directed all aspects of daily life, both private and public. A Jewish family avoided all manner of leaven and ate only matza during Passover because that was the way Jewish people behaved. However, in the late nineteenth century, as Jews began immigrating to America, a lot of them cast off their religious practices and beliefs as remnants of the old country. To become an American, to dress like an American, and to look like an American was their ultimate goal. As Herman Wouk wrote in his novel, *Inside, Outside,* "Jewish immigrants had a saying, 'When the boat is halfway to America, throw overboard your prayer shawl and phylacteries.' To some this meant a release from a galling yoke; to others a sad yielding to the facts of the new world."

Conspicuous displays of religion violated an unwritten code of decorum among those attempting to blend in. Reform Judaism was one way of fitting into the "modern" society of America. By 1880, over ten percent of American synagogues were Reform. It was hard to tell them apart from the nearby Protestant churches. Conservative Judaism came about in the early 1900s as a way to conserve many of the old traditions and practices that Reform Jews had rejected.

Over the course of Yehuda's religious transformation, I came to realize that if it were not for the Orthodox, Judaism would not be the vibrant religion it is today. So when it was time for the panel discussion, not only was I going to participate, I was going to speak out for the Orthodox way of life as a viable option for those who choose to follow it. I needed a refresher course in the whys and wherefores of Orthodoxy. For that I turned to my experts: Yehuda and Penina, Chaim and Shulamit.

Peter and I were scheduled to be in Israel the week before the panel was to take place. If I could come up with the most uncomfortable questions someone might ask me about Orthodoxy, Yehuda and Penina could arm me with the answers in advance. There were so many possible questions that it was hard to come up with the most challenging. And then one came to me.

A friend once told me about a prayer that Orthodox men say every morning. She insisted this was proof positive that Orthodox Judaism is chauvinistic.

"How dare you insinuate that Yehuda is a chauvinist?" I remember saying.

"Just ask him about the prayer," was the reply.

I remembered having once asked Yehuda about the prayer in which he thanked God for not making him a woman, but did not remember his reply. It must have been good enough to satisfy me or I would have pressured him for more.

"Don't try to interview me" or "That's too complicated to explain" had become Yehuda's usual brush-offs. But this time, he waited for me to get my notepad.

Sitting on the chair next to me at the dining room table, with Peter across from us, Yehuda scratched the back of his head.

"What you're asking about isn't really a prayer," he said. "It's a *bracha*."

"That's important?" I asked.

"*brachas* are what we say to thank *Hashem* (God)."

"Like the *bracha* we say over *challah* on *Shabbos*?"

Nodding, he went on, "The *bracha* you're asking about is actually part of a trilogy." Isn't that a Christian concept, I wondered. "Three separate *brachas* in ascending order. In the first I thank *Hashem* for not making me a gentile." He must have noticed my expression because he immediately added, "Not that there's anything wrong with gentiles. But I'd rather be a Jew." He paused so I could take notes. "The second *bracha* thanks *Hashem* for not making me a slave. And the third is for not making me a woman."

"Sure sounds chauvinistic."

"But it's not."

Yehuda then asked if I realized that there are 613 *mitzvot*, commandments, including the Ten Commandments.

I did.

"Do you know why women are excused from all the ones that have to be performed at specific times?"

"Like praying three times a day?"

He smiled, but I could not help wondering where he was going with this.

"I thank *Hashem* for not making me a woman because I'm grateful to be able to become closer to him by performing more *mitzvahs*."

"How do women get closer to God?"

"By nature they're more spiritual than men. That gives them a head start." Yehuda looked at me to make sure his words sank in. "Children are gifts from *Hashem*. Taking care of them brings women even closer to Him."

Watching me expectantly, he waited while I checked my notes. But the paper was blank except for the following words:

3 blessings: not gentile
not servant (slave)
not woman
for oblig. to mitzvas these 3 not have to do

"Maybe it's my jet lag," I said, stifling a yawn. "But I still don't get it."

Hugging me, Yehuda said, "I'll be happy to go over it again as many times as you want."

Peter, who had been uncharacteristically silent, suddenly chimed in, saying he understood it all. Hard to believe he did when I did not.

"Want me to explain it?" Peter asked.

"Maybe later," I said. "Now I need a nap."

"Sweet dreams," Yehuda told me as I walked toward the bedroom.

Waking up an hour later, I found the following note from Peter next to my pillow:

"Religious Jews want to perform as many of the 613 laws as possible. Women are exempt from many of them (especially when raising children and managing their home). Thus men say they are grateful they are not women because as a man they can fulfill more of the 613 laws."

"P. Rosenfeld
2-11-08
Please give proper footnoting to me."

There had to be more to it, so I checked with Penina.

"Judaism is a home-based religion," Penina told me. "The Passover *seder*, the *Shabbos* meals. There's no greater job than wife and mother. Nothing more exalted than the woman's role in serving *Hashem*. Women were happy with their role for 5,000 years. Now they complain that motherhood is underrated and unappreciated. Not Jewish women. We know that raising children is the most important way a woman can serve *Hashem*. It was not until feminism came about that women felt a need to prove themselves. An inferiority complex. In the Bible there are numerous instances in which women are portrayed not only as far more reliable than men in their judgment and in their devotion to *Hashem*, but also with an extra measure of intuitive understanding. When Sarah asked Abraham to send Ishmael off into the wilderness, Abraham resisted until God told him, 'Listen to the voice of your wife, Sarah, for she is a greater prophet than you.'"

"Hold on a sec," I pleaded, struggling to get it all down.

"Men go to *shul*. Women build a home. Men are required to perform all the commandments while women are free to do the holy task of raising children. No one in the world has the capacity for as much loving-kindness as mothers do. Mothers teach their children right from wrong. Mothers may not feel their job is as respectable as if they taught in a school but their home is the place they educate their families." She paused. "I have to remind myself sometimes that I'm actually working toward spiritual perfection by changing dirty diapers."

"That's a new one on me," I told her.

Back in the States, I asked Chaim and Shulamit for their take on the *bracha*. The first thing Chaim did was hand me a copy of an Orthodox prayer book opened to the page on which the *bracha* appears.

"Is this so I can see it in context?" I asked. "So we'll both be on the same page?"

"Read first," Chaim smiled. "Then we'll talk."

When I was done, he made himself comfortable and proceeded to give me his perspective.

"Men and women are different," he said, "Women have the capacity to be more caring, feeling, nurturing, and patient than men. Men can learn to be like that, but these qualities come easier to women. Make sense to you?"

"Sure does," I said.

"Thanks to women's lib, society has a negative view on mothers who stay home and raise their kids. As if it's less important than going out and getting a 'real' job. Remember the movie, "Mr. Mom"? That was not all made up. I'd love to stay home and take care of the kids, but it sure wouldn't be easy."

"But you're a wonderful daddy to Avraham and Aaron," I said.

After smiling his thanks, he went on, "Unlike women, men are not freed from time-bound *mitzvahs*. You think I like waking up to go to a 6:20 *minyan* every morning? I don't. But *Hashem* made me a man, so I deal with it."

"Can't you just pray at home?"

"Some prayers have to be said in *shul*." (A *shul* is a synagogue.)

"But why thank God for not making you a woman."

"Following a rule because it's a rule is better than doing something voluntarily," Chaim went on. "It's human nature to try to resist obligations. I could just thank *Hashem* for making me a man. By saying all three *brachas*, I'm thanking *Hashem* three times instead of just one."

"So?"

"It's a way to get closer to *Hashem*."

"What about women?"

"They're already created closer to *Hashem's* ideal of satisfaction."

"So women are better than men?'

"Yes, when it comes to being closer to *Hashem*."

I looked forward to what Shulamit had to say.

Relaxing on the upholstered rocker in the living room, Shulamit told me. "When it comes to spirituality, women are inherently more connected to *Hashem*. The *Torah* says we have a rich inner world, a unique power to influence people's character."

"By nature of what?" I asked.

"It's so cool that you want to learn all this. Women have *binah*, a special type of deep understanding that brings us closer to *Hashem*." That sounded like women's intuition. "*Hashem* is the Creator of the world. What better way to come closer to him than for a woman to become a creator herself? We give birth and create a young person. We both create and safeguard the world for our children just as *Hashem* safeguards the world for us." I had never thought of childbirth like that. "Women don't need outside reminders to be spiritual, men do." Reminders? "They have to wear *yarmulkes* to remind them that *Hashem* is always above them."

"Orthodox women cover their heads too," I said.

Tucking a few stray hairs into her turquoise scarf, Shulamit said, "But we do that out of modesty. Men need to pray three times a day in shul. We can *daven* if we want. But we don't have to."

"Chaim said he sometimes sees women *davening* on the subway at 9:00 a.m. on their way to work. That's because women are usually too busy taking care of the kids to be required to perform a commandment at a specific time. Right?"

"You got it."

"If we're so special, why do men thank God for not making them a woman?'

"Going through childbirth definitely isn't easy."

"So men are thanking God for not having to go through it?"

"That's how I see it."

This was finally beginning to make some sense.

"So when men say the *bracha* they're not saying women are inferior, are they?"

"Nope," she smiled.

"All this talking that I've been doing about that *bracha*, isn't this a little like learning *Torah*?"

Shulamit's smile broadened.

40

❧❧

The Order of Orders

Judaism does not discourage questions. *Pesach*, Passover, is a case in point. On *Pesach*, we read aloud from the *Haggadah*, a special prayer book, written in the form of questions and answers. The highlight is the recitation of the Four Questions by the youngest child at the table. Whenever I open a *Haggadah*, I remember the mixture of delight and anticipation I felt upon chanting the Four Questions for the first time:

"Mah nishtanah ha-laylah ha-zeh mi-kol ha-laylos? She-b'khol ha-laylos anu okhlin chameytz u-matzah. ha-laylah ha-zeh, kuloh matzah..."

"Why is this night different from all other nights? On all other nights, we eat chametz and matza. Why tonight, only matza?

On all other nights we eat any vegetable. Why tonight, only maror?

On all other nights we don't have to dip even once. Why tonight, twice?

On all other nights we eat sitting or reclining. Why tonight do we recline?"

Little did I know how different that night would become over the course of my life.

The *seders*, the festive *Pesach* meals, of my childhood, took place at Nana's. Many of my relatives traveled at least eight hours to be there. Nana's dining room was so crowded that Pop inevitably was forced to sit on the couch instead of a chair at the head of the table. The *seders* started after sundown and went on long into the evening. I so enjoyed

being with my older cousins—I saw them only a few times a year—
that even as a little girl I had no trouble staying awake.

After the first part of the *Haggadah*, Nana served her family-
famous matza ball soup, sweet and tart carrot *tzimmis*, potato *kugel*
—that she sometimes oversalted—along with the same brisket she
made for *Shabbos*, but that for Passover she tended to overcook. After
dessert, the grownups liked to *schmooze*, chat, so my cousins took me
for a walk. Somehow we always ended up at the pharmacy across the
street just before closing time. Rock candy is made with corn syrup.
And corn is a food Jews are not supposed to eat on *Pesach*. Until I
was in my teens I could not figure out why the rock candy my cousins
bought for me at the pharmacy always tasted better on Passover than
it did during the rest of the year.

When we got back to Nana's, the grownups were almost finished
with the second part of the *Haggadah*. But we were usually in time to
join them in singing *Chad Gadya*, my favorite Passover song, which I
knew by heart.

Nana was getting old by the time Yehuda and Chaim were born, so
Peter and I started hosting *seders* in our home, inviting our friends and
their families to join us. Early on we started skipping the second part of
the *Haggadah*, telling ourselves it was so the kids would not have to stay
up too late. The reality was that after a big meal, the last thing we wanted
to do was sit at the table for a few more hours of prayer.

At Nana's, the adults read the Hebrew portions of the *Haggadah*.
At ours—with the exception of the Four Questions and a few blessings—we read the English because it was easier. As years went by, our
sons started taking a more active role in the *seders*. They seemed to enjoy
showing off the Hebrew they were learning at our synagogue. Though
their lessons were only two afternoons each week, they were each able to
read out loud in Hebrew far more smoothly than Peter or me.

As our sons became more religious, they insisted on including the
second part of *Haggadah*. Peter used to lead the *seders*. Then our sons
took over. Our friends still continued to join us but usually left before
midnight. Our *seders* no longer ended by 10:00 p.m. but dragged on
until at least 2:00 a.m. Peter and I would be nodding off at the table

while our sons would be singing the songs in the *Haggadah* with as much energy as if their day had just begun.

The first time I dozed at the *seder* table, when I woke up, my elbow hurt from resting my head on it. My watch said 1:00 a.m.

Peter was yawning.

"Why can't we stop now?" I heard him say.

Rubbing my eyes, I asked, "What's the big deal if we skip something?"

I don't recall which one of our sons said, "You taught us not to do things half-way."

I sat there, too tired to think of a comeback.

Slowly pushing himself away from the table, Peter said, "I'm going to bed."

Before the words, "Me too" escaped my lips, I reminded myself that *Pesach* was supposed to be a family holiday.

The least Peter and I could do was keep Yehuda and Chaim company at the *seder* table, no matter how long it took. Having religious sons was not in my plans, but since we Jews make up only a tiny portion of the world's population—less than 1% at last count—I had done my best to instill in our sons the feeling that being Jewish is something to be proud of. Too bad Peter had not agreed to enroll Yehuda at a Jewish day school in Albany. As it was, Yehuda did well in public school but didn't make as many Jewish friends as I had hoped.

With more enthusiasm than I actually felt, I said to our sons, "Dad and I would be happy to stay at the *seder* until you're done."

"Thanks, Mom," Yehuda said.

With that, he and Chaim started singing *Chad Gadya*.

Years later, during the first year of Yehuda and Penina's marriage, we were invited to Penina's parents' house for *Pesach*. During the *seder*, the head of the household hides a special piece of matza, called the *afikomen*, which is to be eaten as part of the dessert. It is up to the children to retrieve it from its hiding place. The meal isn't considered complete until everyone eats a bit of the *afikomen*. Yehuda and Chaim never failed to find it after Peter stowed it somewhere near his seat. At the appropriate time, they would present him with the *afikomen*, and, in exchange he would give them a small gift: a few silver dollars or the latest set of Legos they had been asking for. There was never any haggling.

At this *seder*, every adult male had his own *afiikomen*. Five men were involved in this enterprise: Penina's grandfather, father, and older brother, plus Yehuda and Peter. And there were six children: Penina's sister and younger brother and four nieces. Unbeknownst to us, before the *seder* started, the kids decided whose *afikomen* they each were going to hunt down. Penina's eight-year-old niece once refused to return Penina's grandfather's *afikomen* until he agreed to give her a new bicycle.

"Will you settle for one wheel?" the grandfather asked.

Giggling, the girl in question said, "I need two wheels."

"How about just a seat?"

More giggles.

"I need two wheels and a seat."

"Handlebars?"

And so on.

At the end of the bargaining—that went on for fifteen minutes or more—not only did the grandfather agree to a bicycle but also to a helmet and some spending money for any extras. What fun this was not only for those involved, but also for the rest of us.

Next it was Peter's turn. Penina's ten-year-old niece wanted an American Girl doll. With two sons, we had no idea what this was or how much it cost so Peter gave in right away. The girl's mother later apologized to us, saying she had no idea her daughter was going to ask for something so expensive. She offered to buy it herself and say it came from us but we did not take her up on her offer. From Penina, we knew that the only truly expensive gifts her nieces received all year were in exchange for the *afikomens*. In succeeding years, the other girls each picked Peter's *afikomen* and bargained for their own American Girl dolls. Who knew they would someday bring them to Chaim's wedding?

Peter and I stopped spending *Pesach* with Penina's parents a few years after Yehuda and Penina moved to Israel. It was not the same without them. We thought about making our own *seders* again and inviting our friends, but they invited us instead. These *seders*, although enjoyable, were really excuses for eating a big meal. Reading from the *Haggadah* was an afterthought.

After Chaim and Shulamit were married, they started inviting us to their *seders*. What a privilege to see our younger son as a man!

41

A Writing Group for Orthodox Women

A little over a year ago, Penina's mother Malka called to tell me that an Orthodox women's writing group was having its first meeting in her neighborhood. Was I interested? Of course. Did she think they'd let me come to the meeting even though I'm not Orthodox? She saw no reason why not. We usually touched base every few weeks, sharing stories about our mutual grandchildren, but she must have sensed my excitement about the writing group. So instead of chatting, she gave me the number to call and said good-bye.

The woman I spoke to was impressed by my willingness to make the four-hour trip to Brooklyn. Little did she realize that my motivation was not only to improve my writing but also to learn more about Orthodox Jewish women. Did they have the same hopes, dreams, and worries as the rest of us? How much did they know about the secular world? What would they write about?

During a follow-up phone call, I learned that an author named Sarah Shapiro was coming in from Israel to set up this group and a few others in the New York City area.

"Who is she?" I asked.

"The author of wonderful books and short stories about the *frum* world. Hard to believe you haven't read them," I was told. "A few women are joining the group just to meet her."

Googling Sarah Shapiro, I learned that her father was Norman Cousins, the noted author and editor of *The Saturday Review of*

Literature, a magazine I used to enjoy. Accessing some of Ms. Shapiro's work took a bit of hunting, but was worth the effort. She is an incisive, cogent, and articulate author. Most definitely someone I would trust to help me with my own writing.

The next two weeks didn't go by fast enough, but every now and then I was hit by twinges of anxiety. Would the women accept me? Would they let down their guard or treat me as an outsider? I had to take a chance. The opportunity to participate in such a group might not come around again.

Malka suggested staying at her house the evening of the meeting. She and Shloime had a wedding that night, so I planned to skip dinner. But no sooner did Malka open the door to hug me than the tantalizing aroma of broiled salmon wafted in my direction.

"I took the liberty of making dinner for you. Enjoy!" she said before disappearing into her bedroom to get dressed for the wedding. She and I have a lot in common. We both tend to put others' needs before our own.

As it turned out, I was the last to arrive at the meeting. Nineteen women were already seated in the elegantly appointed dining room of the private home when I walked in. Settling into the only empty seat, I noticed all of the women smiling at me. Next to me was Sarah Shapiro, who took less than two minutes to introduce herself to the group and then asked us to do the same.

My fingertips started tingling soon after I picked up my pen—that sometimes happens when I'm nervous—and tried to take notes. Before long, I gave up. Making eye contact with each speaker was more important. The thick Brooklyn accents were a little off-putting, but I did my best to decipher every word that was spoken. I wish I could remember their names, but they spoke too fast.

With the exception of one woman who wore a hat on top of her *sheitel*, the others wore *sheitels* or *tichels*, scarves. Having been told that wearing a hat was not necessary, I did not bother. That made me the only one whose head was bare. *Maybe they won't notice*. At least my black tights, long navy skirt and high-necked aqua sweater did not set me apart.

There were two guidance counselors, one eighth-grade English teacher, a middle school principal, a high school principal, a librarian, the librarian's mother, a playwright for a girls' summer camp, four bookkeepers, one food critic for a local paper, five stay-at-home moms, and one retired foreign language teacher (me). One woman had recently moved from Tennessee. Another was in the process of transcribing her father's wartime experiences from a Yiddish audiotape into English. Our ages ranged from mid-twenties to late sixties. Except for the librarian's mother, I was the oldest. What we all had in common was the desire to share our lives through the written word.

Sarah Shapiro gave us a choice of writing prompts to help us warm up: a conversation, a face in the window, the house we grew up in, a prayer, an embarrassing experience, a betrayal, a turning point in our childhood.

We had been asked to bring along a writing sample that would take no more than a few minutes to read aloud. One woman had written about the various strategies she had tried in dealing with her three-year-old son's temper tantrums. Another woman's piece had to do with the trials of coping with an aging parent. Someone else wondered whether her daughter would ever find a husband. One piece was about the harsh realities of not being able to become pregnant.

When it was my turn, I hesitated, bracing myself, not knowing what kind of reaction my words would receive. No sooner did I open my mouth to speak than my self-confidence started to return. The piece I brought had to do with a conversation I once had with a mother who tried to equate her son's homosexuality with my sons' religious transformation. She thought that we had a lot in common. After I finished reading my piece aloud, the Orthodox women expressed shock and annoyance at the other mother's assumption that homosexuality had anything in common with religious beliefs. I was happy to know my story struck a chord with them.

"You should submit that to *Jewish Action*," one woman called out. I later found out that *Jewish Action* is a quarterly magazine aimed at the Orthodox community.

"Maybe not," another shook her head. "It might be too risqué."

"Try it anyway," someone said.

Another woman had written about an incident that still troubled her twenty years later. Her husband was aware of what had happened but tried to put it out of his mind. So many years had passed, but he still refused to discuss it with her. As this woman read, a depth of emotion seeped into her voice. Everyone in the room winced as she revealed the details of her trauma. It was as powerful a piece of writing as any I have encountered. I wish I could share this woman's story. But I simply cannot. All of us at the table were asked to keep that woman's sacred secret. What I can share was the relief she said she felt as soon as she put her story on paper.

Before the meeting broke up, Sarah Shapiro told us to continue to be brutally honest about our feelings. She suggested we write everyday and keep a notebook for ideas, especially those that come during *Shabbos,* when we're free from the pressures of the work week. She reminded us that sorting through the mundane facts of each day can provide the kernel of an idea to write about.

By the end of the session, I felt encouraged that Jewish publications might be interested in my work. As the only secular woman in the group, many of the others envied my experiences in the secular world, especially my ability to pick up and read whatever I wanted without having to worry about the content. Several said they are very selective when it comes to what they choose to read. Most of their options are found in Judaica stores. Although they frequent the public library, they would never read anything like *Madame Bovary* or *The Scarlet Letter.* Any topic that might be considered risqué was outside their realm.

The writing group surpassed my expectations as a window into the world of Orthodox women. I came away with the insight that despite dressing more modestly than my friends and me, they share the same concerns about family and friends. The workshop confirmed what I already knew. Orthodox Jews are real people. They are firm in their religious beliefs. They lack much that our secular American culture regards as essential to happiness, but they are not that different from us. They are warm and generous, and welcomed me into their own rich world, if only for a night.

42

❦

Only a Few Are Chosen

The other day, Yehuda left a message on our machine saying he wanted to discuss something important with Peter and me. The best time to get us is 6:00 a.m.—with the seven hour time difference, that translates to 1:00 p.m. in Israel. He's rarely home from the *yeshiva* before 10:00 p.m. so I wasn't surprised that we didn't hear from him again for a week. But all the while, I kept wondering what he wanted to tell us. No long ago, he told us that Penina was pregnant with their seventh. Maybe his news was that she's having twins. The last time Yehuda was in the States, he packed up a lot of books for Israel. According to Chaim, the only time someone goes to the trouble of taking such a large supply of Hebrew books with him is when he plans on spending an extended period of time there. Maybe that was what Yehuda wanted to tell us, that he and Penina had decided not to move back to the United States. When I mentioned that to Peter, he assured me I had it all wrong. As it turned out, he was wrong.

When Yehuda and Penina left for Israel seven years ago, they insisted the move would be temporary; only for a year; a place with a warm, dry climate so that his allergies wouldn't bother him so much; and a good *yeshiva* where he could continue his studies. And Penina would not have been interested in him if he hadn't planned to study *Torah* for a few more years before looking for a job.

When was Yehuda going to get a job? Was he going to become a rabbi? How long was this *Torah* learning going to continue? These were ongoing questions. Not sure what he planned to do with his life, he continued to remind us that the decision was his and Penina's; that he was a married man whose wife had a good job; that becoming a *Torah* scholar was a vocation held in high esteem in the world of the Orthodox, so it was not unusual for Penina to work while he studied.

The concept of learning *Torah* as a full-time career was foreign to Peter and me. In our world, both husband and wife work to support their family. We expected Yehuda to get "a real job." I seem to recall that Shloime and Malka agreed with us. I recently came across a print-out of an e-mail from Shloime, who granted me permission to quote him. I give you his words:

> "'Just for the record, there is quite a bit of ambivalence in the *Torah* community about the concept of 'sitting and learning' as a full time career. The rabbis who head the *yeshivas* are all in favor of it. The *yeshivas* are basically geared to produce '*Rosh Yeshivas*' (chief rabbis). Most 'ordinary' people such as myself and my parents like to see people working and earning an honest living and learning on their own time (early mornings and evenings).
>
> "However, almost everyone agrees that there are 'the chosen few' who have the ability, the concentration, and the dedication to rise to great heights. And the world does need rabbis and leaders. These few should stay in learning as long as they possibly can. Penina was looking for one of those 'chosen few' and she found him."

I must have missed this message the first time around, not given it much thought, or filed it away for future reference. Thinking back to all the times Peter tried to push Yehuda into getting "a real job," I cannot help but wonder if things would have been easier for all of us if only Peter and I had paid more attention to Shloime's e-mail.

Penina has many students and Yehuda gets a small stipend from his *yeshiva*. They lead a simple life. They do not crave a lot of "creature comforts." They don't eat out. The only time they have pizza delivered is when we visit. Many of their furnishings—not their beds—are from a used furniture store. They do not own a car. They usually take buses, not taxis, to save money.

The last time I brought up the topic of moving back to the United States, Yehuda told me that both he and Penina are happy living where they are. His learning at the *yeshiva* is going well; she has a lot of friends in their community; her business is thriving. I was not at all happy when Yehuda finally told us that they wanted to buy an apartment in Israel, but it was something I had been expecting.

"I know how much this hurts you," Yehuda said. "But I've got to take care of my family. Jerusalem is the best place for us at this moment in our lives."

"I don't mind telling you how disappointed I am," Peter told him. "You're not being fair to everyone else. Don't your grandparents deserve to have you nearby? And what about Penina's parents? How can you do this to them? They can't afford to visit you as often as we do."

"I know this is painful for you, but it's the right move for us. The price of apartments is going up. Buying one is a good investment."

Yehuda and his family live in an Orthodox community that is somewhat insulated from the rest of Jerusalem. Before Penina agreed to move there, she had to resign herself to the idea of moving away from her friends and neighbors who lived in Jerusalem proper. What finally convinced her was the reality that during their first three years of living in Israel, she and Yehuda lived in at least six different apartments, due to circumstances beyond their control. Constantly packing and unpacking was tiresome. Their children deserved the stability of living in one place for an extended period of time.

When Yehuda discussed the possibility of moving to a larger apartment a few years ago, we told him to go for it. A fourth bedroom meant we could continue to stay with them and not have to move to a hotel when they had more children. So we advised them to take the larger apartment and insisted they let us help out a bit with the rent.

Sometimes, I think we're out of our minds when accepting their desire to continue living in Israel. A recent shooting at a *yeshiva* in

Jerusalem brought this to mind. Seven Jewish families lost their sons. They were killed for learning *Torah. Whoever heard of such a thing?* There are tears in my eyes as I write this.

It is indeed hard to find a place in this world that is completely free from violence; acts of violence abound; students are murdered by other students in our own schools; and add those killed during the commission of everyday crimes. But random acts of violence are a far cry from continued, targeted acts of violence that are inflicted on Israel on a daily basis.

I want my family to be safe. What can I do? Definitely not blasé about the situation in Israel, I am just trying to face the facts. Yehuda and Penina are adults who are well aware of what is going on. But that does not stop me from feeling grateful to hear their voices whenever we call to make sure they are okay.

Now that Chaim is an adult with a family of his own, I asked him how he felt about Yehuda and Penina living in Israel.

"It's scary when things happen," Chaim told me. "But you have to live. You can't run away."

I wondered if he would feel any different if he were talking about his own son and not his brother, but he said he would feel the same.

Thinking back to when our sons went to college, it was Peter who insisted they attend schools no more than four hours away from home so they would have no problem coming home for a weekend and we could easily visit them. That's the reason Yehuda went to Princeton and Chaim went to the University of Pennsylvania. I would have let them go to California, if they had wanted. They needed to learn to take care of themselves and become independent.

"Dad and I want you to do what's right for your family." I told Yehuda. "If buying an apartment in Israel is the right thing, then do it,"

"Thanks, Mom. I knew I could count on you."

Was there something wrong with me, I wondered. Didn't I love our sons as much as Peter did? Not only wasn't I as upset as Peter, I felt relieved. The pressure was off. Preparing for Yehuda's family to visit us is not easy. As much as I want to be with them, it is hard to relax when they're here. The last time was a year ago, but I still remember how stressful it was—shopping at the supermarket two hours away from our home beforehand, and then Yehuda checking to make sure everything met his specifications.

Despite the plane ride and the jet lag, it is much easier going to Israel than having them visit us. As a matter of fact, I'd been wondering how I'd manage with them visiting us on a regular basis when they moved back to the United States. Now I don't have to worry about that for a while.

Yehuda does not know—and I never plan to tell him—but whenever Peter and I visit him and Penina in Israel, we're ready to come home after only a few days. We feel welcome in their home but their way of life is not ours. They have neither television nor radio and don't even bother with the newspaper. The only newspapers available in their community are in Hebrew. If anything important happens, Yehuda says someone will tell him about it. That's not the way Peter and I do things. At home, we enjoy daily delivery of *The New York Times* which we each read from cover to cover. In order to keep abreast with the rest of the world while visiting Yehuda and his family, we have no choice but to take a fifteen-minute taxi ride to the tourist area of Jerusalem to buy an English-language newspaper.

Although we love spending time with our grandchildren, they have their own schedules. Yehuda gets up early and prays at a nearby synagogue. Penina wakes the kids and gets them dressed. They all have breakfast together when Yehuda gets back. He puts the older ones on the bus to school and pre-school and then goes to *yeshiva*, sometimes not coming home until after they are in bed. During our visits, Yehuda makes a point of coming home for either lunch or dinner or both. To make up for the time he misses at the *yeshiva*, he stays up late at night studying what he did not get to do during the day.

As the conversation drifted to the type of apartment they plan to buy, Yehuda surprised me by asking if I would like to have my own room for writing. Perhaps he was returning my love and support for his transformation.

Yehuda and Penina seem to have reached a kind of closure. They haven't officially made *aliyah* (the act of becoming Israeli citizens), probably because they know how upset we'd be. Even so, they keep renewing their visas year after year. But now that they want to buy an apartment in Israel, we do not believe they will ever move back to the United States.

No matter. Our hearts will always follow our sons, whether in Israel or the United States.

Over the years, Peter and I strove to let our sons become individuals. Yehuda and Chaim have each found their niche. I would never begrudge either of them the paths they have chosen. And I could not be more proud of the men they have become.